Law for Doctors:
principles and practicalities

Second Edition

Law for Doctors: principles and practicalities

Second Edition

MA Branthwaite MD FRCP FFARCS

Barrister, Lincoln's Inn

Formerly Consultant Physician and Anaesthetist
Royal Brompton Hospital, London

Associate Member, Crown Office Chambers
One Paper Buildings, Temple, London

Formerly Assistant Deputy Coroner
Inner London (South)

AND

NW Beresford MB ChB LLB

Barrister, Lincoln's Inn

Senior Adviser in Clinical Risk
Royal Brompton and Harefield NHS Trust, London

Formerly General Practitioner
North Lochs Medical Practice, Isle of Lewis

The ROYAL
SOCIETY *of*
MEDICINE
PRESS *Limited*

▶ Preface

Changes in legal procedure introduced in response to Lord Woolf's report into civil justice are now well integrated into practice and so require less emphasis in an introductory text. Some chapters in this new edition have therefore been condensed or eliminated. New material has been introduced to amplify the section on confidentiality and the disclosure of records, and the text has otherwise been updated to incorporate new statute and caselaw since April 2000. To the best of our knowledge, the law is stated correctly as at October 1st 2002.

MA Branthwaite
NW Beresford

London, November 2002

▶ Preface to First Edition

Few sources of medical law are easily accessible to medical practitioners, and research is hindered by unfamiliar legal terminology and style. And yet the law is impinging on medical practice ever more frequently and creates anxiety which is exacerbated by the impotence of ignorance. 'Legal paternalism' is accepted, often gratefully, but is no more appropriate today than its medical equivalent in patient care. This book sets out to provide health care professionals, particularly doctors, with sufficient understanding of the law to alleviate as far as possible those elements of concern which are founded on uncertainty, to assist them to participate more fully in discussions and decisions on cases with which they are involved and, above all, to have some idea of what to expect, be they required to assist the court or face legal action themselves. The content is restricted to those aspects of the law which involve medical practitioners most often.

The style of a medical rather than a legal textbook has been adopted. Case reports (legal authorities) are identified numerically and collected together at the end of each chapter as references. They are also listed alphabetically in a Table of Cases at the beginning of the book, preceded by a key to the accepted abbreviations for relevant series. Wherever possible, the citation in Medical Law Reports has been chosen in preference to other legal sources. This series began in 1989 and is available at the library of the Royal Society of Medicine, as is a textbook of medical caselaw incorporating synopses of the most important actions reported before 1990. Statutes referred to in the text are listed after the Table of Cases. There is a glossary of legal terms before the index, and more detailed sources of medical law are identified at the end of chapter one. In accordance with section 6 of the Interpretation Act 1978, masculine pronouns are used throughout to indicate persons of either gender.

To the best of my knowledge and belief, the law is stated correctly as at April 1 2000.

MA Branthwaite
London, April 2000

Contents

▶ Law Reports — Abbreviations

AC . . . . Appeal Cases
(Decisions of the House of Lords)
All ER . . . . All England Reports
BMLR . . . . Butterworths Medical Law Reports
Crim LR . . . . Criminal Law Reports
ECHR . . . . European Court of Human Rights
JP . . . . Justice of the Peace Reports
LJKB . . . . Law Journal Reports, King's Bench
Lloyd's Rep Med . . . . Lloyd's Law Reports: Medical
(Continuation since 1998 of Medical Law Reports)
Med LR . . . . Medical Law Reports
QBD (or KBD) . . . . Queen's (or King's) Bench Division
(Queen's Bench Division of High Court)
WLR . . . . Weekly Law Reports

Law Reports sought electronically are often identified by year and court number. Current numbering denotes the jurisdiction and court, thus [2001] EWCA is a case heard in the Court of Appeal (England and Wales) in 2001.

▶ Table of Cases

Entries identify the chapter and the numbered reference within it.

▶ Table of Statutes

The reference is to the page on which each Act is mentioned

►1
Structure and sources of English law

Similarities between medicine and the law

Medicine and the law share a number of common characteristics. The practical applications of medicine divide broadly into medicine (physic) and surgery, the law into civil and criminal practice. Practitioners of either discipline require prolonged training, with academic (pre-clinical) studies preceding vocational (clinical) training, followed by a period of quasi-apprenticeship (pupil or house officer). Specialisation is common after full registration (call to the Bar) and practitioners may choose to adopt a continuing professional relationship with clients (GP or solicitor), or a consultative role sought only in particular circumstances (specialist or counsel).

Medicine and surgery both divide into sub-specialities and so too do civil and criminal law. Tort, or inter-personal wrong-doing short of criminality, is a sub-division of civil law which includes 'wrongs' such as negligence, nuisance, defamation and trespass to the person. Another sub-division, the law of contract, deals with disputes arising from legally enforceable agreements, although contracts for the sale of land are considered separately again. The boundaries of these legal sub-divisions are not always clear cut, any more than they are in medicine.

Most litigation against medical practitioners consists of claims for the tort of negligence, although private practice also spawns claims for breach of contract. As in medicine, there is some overlap even between the primary sub-divisions – for example, gastro-intestinal haemorrhage can be managed medically or surgically. Similarly assault and battery can constitute either a criminal offence, or the civil wrong (tort) of trespass to the person. In exceptional cases, negligence is deemed so gross as to warrant prosecution as a criminal offence (see chapter 10).

The nature of legal proceedings determines the location for any hearing or trial, the status of the presiding judicial officer, and the degree of formality to be adopted in court. These practical aspects are considered in more detail in chapters 5, 9 and 10.

Differences between medicine and the law – the role of caselaw

The similarities set out above are matched by significant differences, the most important being sources of knowledge and the way in which these are applied. Modern medicine is founded on scientific study, which may be incomplete or even erroneous, but which seeks to establish principles which can then be applied to individual cases. Case reports are no more than interesting curiosities: they are not binding truths. By contrast, English common law is built upon caselaw – the body of decided judgments in individual cases which together form legal principles. These principles are then applied in subsequent cases unless the new matter can be distinguished on its facts from all the preceding decisions, or new and cogent argument for change can be advanced. A single case report, sometimes of considerable antiquity, can suffice to secure a contested point unless that decision has been specifically overruled by a more recent and authoritative judgment.

Legal precedent

This term describes the binding power of previous decisions on the determination of subsequent, similar cases. It is intended to secure parity of treatment. Decisions in the High Court are binding upon lower courts such as those presided over by magistrates and coroners, and are usually, but not necessarily, followed in subsequent High Court judgments. Decisions by the Appellate Courts (Court of Appeal and House of Lords) are binding on all lower courts and, although the House of Lords has a power to reverse a decision of its own, this is only invoked very rarely.

Statutory law

Superimposed upon common law – the legacy of decided cases – are the provisions of statute. Statutes are Acts of Parliament brought into force on a designated date after completion of a series of procedural steps, culminating in the grant of Royal assent. Such parliamentary legislation may define an issue not previously subject to exploration in the courts, or it may consolidate principles established at common law into a legally-binding statute. Many Acts create a power to delegate subsidiary decision-making to a designated minister, local authority or other official. This 'subordinate legislation' can be actioned swiftly and simply when need arises, to make changes to detail as distinct from principle. If there are concerns that the power has been used improperly, application can be made by properly interested persons for judicial review. This means that ministerial decisions are subject to review by the courts – ie the judiciary. This contrasts with Acts of Parliament which can only be rescinded or amended by further legislation. There is no power for an English parliament to limit the discretion of its successors.

European Law

The United Kingdom joined the European Community in 1973. The enabling legislation (European Communities Act 1972) requires that all provisions of Community law intended to take direct effect in the UK shall do so, whether made before or after the Act came into force. This means that despite the centuries-old tradition of the absolute sovereignty of Parliament, UK Acts are, from that time, subject to Community law. When called upon to interpret statutory law, the domestic courts must do so in conformity with EC law. Matters of conflict are referred to the European Court of Justice, usually after a series of domestic appeals ultimately reaching the House of Lords. Once the European Court has given its decision on the specific point of law, the case is returned to the English courts for final determination in the light of the European ruling.

The Human Rights Act 1998 incorporates into English law the European Convention for the Protection of Human Rights and Fundamental Freedoms and came into force in October 2000. The UK was an original signatory to the Convention in 1950 but did not incorporate its terms into domestic law. Claimants seeking to assert a right under the Convention could only do so by application to the European Court of Human Rights and Fundamental Freedoms. They can now take action through the English courts, although the European Court remains the final arbiter for those who remain dissatisfied.

The law in Scotland and Northern Ireland

English common law applies in England and Wales. It is similar in principle in Northern Ireland but there are some differences too, for example, proceedings in the coroners court. The law in Scotland is different in both structure and principle and has more in common with the continental system known, confusingly, as civil law. Fortunately the differences of principle between English and Scots law relating to clinical negligence are minor and are not considered here.

Legislative basis for the regulation of health care

A series of statutes defines the components and organisation of the NHS. The most important current statutes are the National Health Service Act 1977, the NHS and Community Care Act 1990, the NHS Primary Care Act of 1997, the Health Act 1999 and Health and Social Care Act 2001. Regulations governing the availability and prescribing of medicinal products are also enshrined in statute and so too are the powers to register and regulate the performance of medical practitioners. A number of other statutes apply to specific aspects of medical practice, eg assisted reproduction, transplantation. In the recent past, the government has responded to public concern about the NHS by establishing a number of new statutory authorities. These include the National Institute for Clinical Excellence (NICE), Commission for Health Improvement (CHI), National Patient Safety Agency (which registers accidents and near misses) and the National Clinical Assessment Authority (to supervise the performance of possibly under-performing doctors). Further legislation is before Parliament (NHS Reform and Health Care Professions Bill) or in draft form (Medical Act 1983 (Amendment) Order 2002) with the aim of implementing the government's intention to secure greater public involvement in health care decision-making and professional regulation.

Sources of legal authority

Compendia of statutes and statutory instruments are published and updated regularly. Legislation introduced recently is also available without restriction on the internet. Caselaw is available in published series, some of which are available electronically in whole or in part, but only to subscribers. Recent important judgments of the High Court and Appellate courts are posted on the internet where they can be identified by name or court number.

Law reports – referred to as 'authorities' – are published both in official series, identified according to the court in which the hearing was held, and unofficial series which are more eclectic. Accepted abbreviations are used to identify the series; those used here are explained in front of the Table of Cases. The year of publication is often an essential identifying feature and, if so, is entered in square brackets []. If the date is no more than an ancillary to identification, for example where there are consecutive journal numbers, the year is quoted in round brackets (). The date precedes the abbreviation for the series, followed by the page number, often with a subsidiary reference to a particular passage in the judgment. Many series include a head-note or summary. These are not part of the official judgment and should be used cautiously. There are also 'casebooks' containing abstracts of reports on specific legal topics, often accompanied by useful and authoritative comment. A small number of long-established textbooks, usually referred to by the name of the original author, also have status as legal authority and may be quoted in court. The national press, particularly *The Times* Law Reports, includes some detailed and authoritative reports which are accepted as legal authority if the case is not reported elsewhere.

Reports of medical caselaw have been available as a single series since 1989, first published by BMP (Business and Medical Publications) then without change of title by Oxford University Press and, since 1998, with a new title and format as one of the Lloyd's legal report series. A less widely consulted series is Butterworth's Medical Law Reports. Cases before the late 1980s must be sought in non-specialist series. Inquests are not reported formally but appeals arising from them appear in Justice of the Peace Reports and sometimes in the independent series as well.

Access to Sources of Legal Authority

www.hmso.gov.uk   full text of UK legislation since 1988

www.courtservice.gov.uk   access to recently decided cases

www.bailii.org   British and Irish Legal Information Institute; very comprehensive source of both statute and caselaw

www.parliament.the-stationery-office.co.uk Decisions of the House of Lords; Parliamentary procedures and publications

www.lcd.gov.uk   legal procedure; links to other sources of legal information

www.context.co.uk   caselaw (also available on compact disc); subscription only

www.lawreports.co.uk   Incorporated Council of Law Reporting; Daily Law Notes

www.echr.coe.int   decisions of the European Court of Human Rights

Textbooks on medical law include

Jones MA.	Medical Negligence, 2nd Edition. Sweet & Maxwell, 1996. 3rd Edition scheduled for December 2002.
Kennedy I & Grubb A. (Eds)	Principles of Medical Law. Oxford University Press, 1998. An annual update is published as a cumulative supplement.
Matthews P & Foreman J.	Jervis on the Office and Duties of Coroners, 11th Edition. Sweet & Maxwell, 1993. Regular supplements also available. 12th Edition scheduled for December 2002.
Powers MJ & Harris N. (Eds)	Clinical Negligence, 3rd Edition. Butterworths, 2000.

Casebooks on medical law include

Kennedy I & Grubb A.	Medical Law: text and materials, 3rd Edition. Butterworths, 2000.
Knapman P & Powers MJ.	Sources of Coroners' Law. Barry Rose, 1999.
Nelson-Jones R & Burton F.	Medical Negligence Caselaw. 1st Ed Fourmat Publishing, 1990. 2nd Ed Butterworths, 1995.
Stauch M, Wheat K.	Sourcebook on Medical Law. Cavendish Publishing, 1998. 3rd Edition (Stauch, Tingle & Wheat) 2002.

▶2

Principles of negligence; duty and standard of care

Legal basis for claims arising from clinical practice

Clinical negligence, a term used in preference to medical negligence to encompass actions against all health professionals, is a sub-section of the law of tort, a generic term for civil wrong-doing. The legal criteria for a finding of negligence are

▶ the existence of a duty of care owed by one person to another

▶ breach of the duty of care

▶ foreseeable injury occurring as a consequence of the breach.

All three elements of the test must be fulfilled if the claimant is to succeed[1].

Private medical practice generates claims founded on breach of contract as well as negligence[2]. A contract is an agreement creating obligations recognised and enforceable by law. It requires

▶ offer

▶ acceptance

▶ consideration – 'the price for which the promise is bought'.

No consideration passes directly between NHS patient and the practitioner or treating hospital. There is no legally enforceable, individual contract[3]. Claims alleging wrongful medical practice within an NHS hospital are therefore virtually always brought in tort. By contrast, claims arising in private practice are often brought in both contract and tort. However, the allegations of wrong-doing (misfeasance) cited as the elements of the tort or contractual default are often identical.

Parties to the action

Surviving adult patients of sound mind who seek redress for perceived clinical error take legal action in their own name. Actions on behalf of children (below 18 years) and those without the necessary mental capacity are brought in their name by a nominated and court-approved 'litigation friend'. Actions arising from the death of a patient are brought by the executor or administrator and often encompass a claim for damages on behalf of the estate of the deceased as well as a claim for financial support for the deceased's dependants.

Actions in negligence lie against the person or persons who owed the duty of care. Institutions such as hospitals can be identified as 'persons' for legal purposes and, since 1990, NHS hospitals have carried vicarious liability for medical as well as other employed staff. It is therefore now usual for the trust to be cited as the defendant whereas actions against general practitioners still lie against the individual. Similarly, private practitioners are either pursued individually or are identified as a co-defendant with a private hospital. Claims brought against more than one defendant raise conflict between them and occasionally a defendant may seek to transfer responsibility for an adverse outcome to a third party (a 'part 20 claim'). These conflicts complicate the legal process but do not undermine the application of legal principle.

Other factors which affect conduct of an action are the value and complexity of the claim and how the parties are funded (see chapters 4 and 5).

Duty of care

The professional obligation of doctors to their patients suffices to found a common law duty of care, reinforced within the National Health Service by the provisions of health service legislation. Sometimes however a doctor's primary duty is to some other individual or organisation, for example, medical examinations for the purposes of employment or insurance[4]. Here the doctor-patient relationship does not exist in conventional terms but the practitioner still has a duty to avoid causing harm. Occasional differences exist between professional and legal obligations, for example, if a child dies during the course of medical treatment, there is a *professional* duty to explain to parents the reasons for and circumstances of the death[5]. However the giving of such information does not create a *legal* duty of care because it does not found a doctor-patient relationship and there is no free-standing duty of candour[6]. There is some scope for claims by individual patients against public services[7], and statutory duties arise from the provision of products to the public[8].

Standard of care

At English law the standard required of medical practitioners is determined by judicial analysis of professional opinion. A doctor is not to be deemed negligent if acting in accordance with the opinion of a responsible body of medical practitioners, skilled and practised in that art[9]. This traditional *'Bolam'* test, so named from the case in which the principle was first enunciated, has been refined more recently by a requirement that medical opinion on which the court is invited to rely must also be 'reasonable', in other words it must be formulated on the basis of a considered evaluation of the risks and benefits associated with a particular procedure and thus be capable of withstanding logical analysis[10]. When expert opinion conflicts, the judge is not permitted merely to prefer one opinion to another but must decide between them by assessing their rationality. However, the court will be slow to reject the sincerely held views of distinguished experts, and due consideration is also given to the different standards which may apply to sub-specialities[11], even though numerically small. Finally and very importantly, the standard to be determined is that which applied at the time of the events in question, *not* at the time of trial[12].

In some instances, guidelines or protocols are cited as a means of defining proper standards, a trend which can be expected to escalate as the National Institute for Clinical Excellence makes recommendations. Important though such guidelines are, legally as well as in practice, they are better considered as indicative of an accepted course of practice rather than the final arbiter of professional standards. Any alternative would stifle the progress of medicine. However, if legal action is brought because harm results from transgression of guidelines or protocols *without good reason*, the claimant is very likely to succeed.

The role of the hospital

The Health Act 1999 imposes a *statutory* duty on Health Authorities, Primary Care Trusts and NHS Trusts to monitor and improve the quality of health care, and establishes the Commission for Health Improvement to inform, advise and review this function. Until this legislative intervention, the basis for imposing liability on a hospital rested on the common law (decided cases), and the principle that an employing authority is vicariously responsible for the negligent actions of its staff[13]. The primary duty is to patients. The personal welfare of staff is included[14], but the duty does not extend to unidentified third parties harmed by the patient of a hospital[15].

Although the court may sympathise with a junior doctor called upon to undertake tasks beyond his competence, the legal position is that hospitals should have in place systems and staff with sufficient experience and expertise to ensure an appropriate standard of care is provided to all patients[16-18]. This must be right from the perspective of the patient but raises obvious difficulties when financial or human resources are restricted. Claims based upon failure to provide a service at all because of insufficient funding are less likely to succeed and, in general, the courts are reluctant to interfere with decisions, taken in good faith, on the allocation of scarce resources[19]. However, 'blanket bans' on a particular procedure have been challenged successfully[20], as has a decision to close a specialist unit, albeit with criticism directed to the procedure rather than the principle[21]. Actions of this nature seek a remedy for alleged maladministration, not compensation for negligently-inflicted personal injury. The appropriate legal process is therefore not an action in tort but *Judicial Review* – a procedure available, with leave, in carefully defined circumstances and to 'properly interested persons'. The Human Rights Act came into force in October 2000. Allegations of contravention of rights protected under the European Convention have since succeeded in the English courts in the context of applications under the mental health legislation and in disciplinary proceedings against medical practitioners (see chapter 8). There has been little effect on the delivery of health care, even in the context of decisions to withhold or withdraw treatment (see chapter 10). It seems unlikely that Article 2, the right to life, could be used to impose an obligation on the NHS to provide medical care in all cases where life might otherwise be endangered.

References

1. Barnett v Chelsea & Kensington HMC [1969] 1QB 428; 2 WLR 422.
   Casualty officer declined to attend three nightwatchmen who were vomiting after drinking tea; one died later from arsenical poisoning. Claim failed. Breach of duty established but no causation – man would have died anyway.
2. Dyer C. Triplets' parents win right to damages for extra child. BMJ 2000 321:1305.
   Successful claim in contract. Three embryos rather than the two agreed were implanted.
3. Reynolds v The Health First Medical Group [2000] Lloyd's Rep Med 240.
   Attempt to circumvent the rules of negligence by asserting a contractual obligation between GP and patient, with NHS capitation fee as consideration. Claim struck-out: the relationship between doctor and patient is statutory.
4. R v Croydon HA [1998] Lloyd's Rep Med 44.
   Failure to diagnosis pulmonary hypertension on a pre-employment chest X-ray. Breach of duty admitted but obligations assumed by the radiologist did not extend to claimant's private life (decision to have a child). See also *Kapfunde v Abbey National & Dr D Daniel [1999] 2 Lloyd's Rep Med 48*. Occupational health report adverse to claimant's application for employment. No duty of care by practitioner; no vicarious liability by employer.

5. General Medical Council: Good Medical Practice 2001 para 23.
Paragraphs 22–23 set out duty to disclose information when an adverse incident occurs.

6. Powell & Another v Boladz *et al* [1998] Lloyd's Rep Med 116.
Doctor-patient relationship not established if practitioner treating a patient who has died informs relatives what happened. Parents of deceased child had no cause of action for psychiatric injury attributed to alleged cover-up.

7. Kent v Griffiths, Roberts and London Ambulance Service [2000] Lloyd's Rep Med 109.
Asthmatic patient suffered respiratory arrest and brain damage during prolonged wait for an emergency ambulance. Judgment, solely against the LAS, was upheld on appeal.

8. A and Ors v The National Blood Authority and Others [2001] Lloyd's Rep Med 187.
Successful claim by patients infected with Hepatitis C during blood transfusion. The Authority was held responsible under the terms of the Consumer Protection Act 1987 in compliance with the European Union Product Liability Directive of 1985.

9. Bolam v Friern Hospital Management Committee [1957] 1 WLR 583.
Claimant suffered fractures during ECT administered without muscle relaxants, a technique endorsed at the time by a 'responsible body of medical opinion'. Test for breach of duty set out by McNair J in directions to jury.

10. Bolitho v City & Hackney HA [1998] Lloyd's Rep Med 26.
Negligent failure to attend a child's respiratory crisis. Court is not necessarily bound by expert opinion. Support by distinguished experts will usually demonstrate reasonableness of an opinion but if, in rare cases, expert opinion is incapable of withstanding logical analysis, judge is entitled to find it is not reasonable or responsible.

11. Defreitas v O'Brien & Another [1993] 4 Med LR 281.
Exploratory spinal surgery in absence of clear clinical or radiological indications to operate. Spinal surgeons deemed to form a category of specialism separate and apart from other orthopaedic and neurosurgeons.

12. Roe v Ministry of Health [1954] 2 WLR 915.
Paraplegia following spinal anaesthesia; ampoules stored in phenol which leached through invisible cracks in the glass. The claim failed: must not look at 1947 accident with 1954 spectacles. (Cause identified & reported in 1951).

13. Cassidy v Ministry of Health [1951] 1 All ER 574.
Surgery and splinting for Dupuytren's contracture; severe post-operative pain; flexion deformity of four fingers. Hospital responsible for adverse outcome, however caused, through its duty to appoint responsible staff.

14. Ogden v Airedale HA [1996] 7 Med LR 153.
Faulty working conditions permitted Radiographer to become sensitised to X-ray chemicals, developing asthma. Awarded damages for his condition, loss of earnings, loss of chosen career and loss of job security.

15. Palmer v Tees HA, Hartlepool & East Durham NHS Trust [1999] Lloyds Rep Med 351.
Psychotic patient murdered a child and mutilated her body a year after hospital discharge. Alleged to have told staff of sexual feelings towards children and that a child would be murdered. Claim on behalf of child and mother struck out – insufficient proximity between hospital and unknown victim to found a duty of care.

16. Wilsher v Essex AHA [1988] AC 1074.
Failure by junior doctor in special care baby unit to recognise misplaced umbilical artery catheter. Health Authority *may be* directly liable to patient for failing to provide sufficient qualified and competent medical staff.

17. Bull v Devon AHA [1993] 4 Med LR 117.
Birth asphyxia in second twin. Health Authority liable for failure to provide and implement efficient system for alerting appropriate staff on call to an impending emergency.

18. Robertson v Nottingham HA [1997] 8 Med LR 1.
Brain damaged infant – foetal distress before onset of labour. Health Authority had a non-delegable duty to establish proper systems of care and can be liable for a 'systems failure'.

19. **R v Cambridge HA** *ex parte* **B (A Minor) [1995] 6 Med LR 250.**
    Decision not to provide unproven treatment for relapse of leukaemia in a child. Court is not the arbiter of merit. Health Authority is legally charged with making decision and is not to be required to present accounts.
20. **NW Lancs HA v A, D & G. [1999] Lloyd's Rep Med 399.**
    Policy not to fund gender reassignment surgery extra-contractually, other than in very exceptional cases, was 'almost a blanket ban'. Rationing accepted as inevitable but must be based on proper assessment of competing need.
21. **R v NW Thames RHA** *et al ex parte* **Daniels [1993] 4 Med LR 364.**
    Health Authority erred in failing to consult interested parties before closing a bone marrow transplant unit *but* no public law remedy was granted because none would have benefited the applicant.

▶3

Foreseeability and causation

The third limb of the test for negligence is itself tripartite. The claimant must establish that

▶ foreseeable

▶ injury

▶ occurred as a result of the breach of the duty of care.

Foreseeability

Complications arising in the course of medical treatment are sometimes wholly unexpected. In legal terms however, an injury is deemed to be a foreseeable consequence of the negligent act if *damage of that general nature* can be foreseen. Thus although anterior spinal artery syndrome would not be cited as a specific risk of induced hypotension during anaesthesia, injury caused by under-perfusion of major organs – including nervous tissue – *is* a foreseeable consequence[1]. Such a complication was therefore deemed to lie within the risk created by a technique of hypotensive anaesthesia considered negligent, despite publication of a large series in a peer-reviewed journal.

Injury

Actions in negligence are brought to secure compensation for harm suffered as a result of a wrongful act. Without an injury causally related to the tort, there is no basis for a claim. This contrasts with actions in battery where the mere fact of unlawful (ie non-consensual) touching warrants compensation, whether or not injury has occurred as a consequence.

Injury which founds a claim for damages can be physical, mental or economic. However, the courts are more willing to compensate physical rather than either mental or economic injury. The victim of a negligent act who suffers psychiatric injury in circumstances where personal injury of some kind is reasonably foreseeable is deemed a 'primary victim' and is entitled to compensation. Conversely, a claimant who suffers psychiatric injury from witnessing the consequences of negligence is a 'secondary victim' and can only recover if able to show a close emotional bond with the victim, proximity in time and place to the accident or its immediate aftermath, and reasonable foreseeability that an onlooker of normal fortitude would suffer mental distress resulting in psychiatric illness[2]. Economic loss which is consequent upon negligently inflicted physical or mental injury, for example, loss of earnings or costs of care, is recoverable. However the courts are reluctant to award damages for pure economic loss. In a recent decision[3], the House of Lords rejected the previously accepted view that the costs of bringing up a child conceived as a result of a negligent sterilisation can be recovered as part of a 'personal injury'. In a series of cases challenging this decision, it has been held that the additional costs of bringing up a disabled child are recoverable[4] and so too are costs incurred by a disabled mother[5]. No distinction is to be drawn between wrongful conception (eg failed sterilisation) or wrongful birth (eg failure to diagnose or warn of possible fetal abnormality). However, pure economic loss by the mother beyond pregnancy and childbirth (loss of employment during child-rearing) has been deemed irrecoverable[6].

Causation of injury

An adverse outcome from medical treatment, even when unexpected, does not suffice to establish a finding of clinical negligence. There must be a causal link with breach of duty. This means it is necessary to establish that the adverse outcome would not have occurred as a result of the natural progression of disease, and was not a foreseeable and accepted complication of treatment carried out to the highest possible standard. Once again the courts rely upon expert medical opinion but, when considering causation rather than breach of duty, evidence from the most recent sources can be adduced. However, causation arguments founded on clinical belief and practice which are *not* substantiated by scientific studies may fail[7]. Sometimes a negligent act is no more than a contributory factor in determining an adverse outcome. Then the court will endeavour to identify and award compensation proportional to that element of the injury[8]. However, if the negligently-caused element of the injury cannot be distinguished, the claimant can succeed in full provided the negligence made a 'material contribution' – in other words was more than *de minimis*[9,10]. In exceptional cases the courts will discount the sum awarded in compensation to reflect contributory negligence by the patient[11].

Injury caused by failure to act

Here the court is faced with a hypothetical situation: what would have been the outcome had there not been a negligent failure to act? In some cases this requires evaluation of the natural progression of untreated disease and, after hearing expert evidence, the judge will make a finding of 'fact' – legal fact – as to what would have occurred but for the negligence. If the adverse outcome is deemed to have been determined before the negligent act, or to have been more likely than not in any event, then the claim fails outright – there is no recovery for the lost chance[12]. However, if there was a greater than 50% chance of a good outcome but for the negligent failure to act, the claimant succeeds and damages are calculated according to the magnitude of the lost chance[13]. There is currently a move towards accepting that loss of less than even a 50% chance should found a successful claim in tort, in proportion to the magnitude of the lost opportunity[14].

A further difficulty is created if the negligent failure to act does not have agreed consequences. Thus if a practitioner fails to attend a patient, the court must determine what *that individual practitioner* would have done if properly attending, and thereafter consider what the practitioner *should* have done if acting in accordance with a responsible body of medical opinion[15,16]. The first question is one of fact. The second requires judicial appraisal of professional opinion.

The burden and standard of proof

It is incumbent on the claimant to establish his case[17]. First the facts must be established and thereafter the successful claimant must satisfy the judge on all three elements of negligence – existence of a duty, breach of duty, and foreseeable injury occurring as a result. The facts may be a matter of contention between the parties, particularly if contemporaneous notes are inadequate, missing, or contain obvious alterations suggesting late amendment. If there is conflict and the matter reaches court, the judge is responsible for making a determination of 'fact' in the light of the evidence presented and his view of the credibility of the witnesses. On causation of injury, the claimant need only establish to the satisfaction of the judge that the adverse outcome was causally related to the alleged negligence *on the balance of probabilities.* This is a far less stringent test than *beyond reasonable doubt* which is the standard required by criminal law.

Res ipsa loquitur

'The thing speaks for itself'. This aphorism is merely a means of drawing an inference of negligence and seeks to imply the adverse outcome is such that no other explanation is tenable. It is sometimes pleaded on behalf of a claimant who cannot know what, in fact, transpired – such as cardiac arrest occurring during general anaesthesia. The defendant must then adduce evidence to rebut the presumption of negligence by offering a plausible, non-negligent explanation. There is no obligation on the defendant to prove the non-negligent explanation was the more likely cause of the catastrophe. It may also be possible to refute the inference of negligence by satisfying the judge that proper care *was* exercised and that the adverse outcome was either extremely rare or impossible to explain in the light of current knowledge[18].

The incomplete case

The requirement to prove a causal link between adverse outcome and breach of duty often presents an insuperable hurdle to the claimant bringing action in clinical negligence. This can be so even when breach of duty has been admitted by the defendant. Many patients have difficulty understanding why their claim has failed when breach of duty is clear, obvious or even admitted. However the legal process is 'all or none' and there is no legally enforceable remedy for breach of duty unless consequential injury can also be established. Alternative dispute resolution may permit exploration of alternatives to an award of damages and is considered in chapter 5.

References

1. Hepworth v Kerr [1995] 6 Med LR 139.
   Anterior spinal artery thrombosis attributed to excessive and unduly prolonged induced hypotension during general anaesthesia. Injury was but a variant of the foreseeable and within the risk created by the negligence.
2. Page v Smith [1996] AC 155.
   House of Lords decision restricting the circumstances in which an onlooker ('secondary victim') can secure compensation for psychiatric injury caused by witnessing distressing events.

3. **McFarlane v Tayside Health Board [2000] Lloyd's Rep Med 1.**
Pain and inconvenience of child-bearing arising from negligent failure of sterilisation is to be compensated but the costs of rearing the child are not recoverable. House of Lords decision reversing earlier caselaw.

4. **Groom v Selby [2002] Lloyd's Rep Med 1.**
Negligent failure to diagnose pregnancy soon after a sterilisation procedure resulted in delivery of a premature child, thereby deemed unduly prone to infection. Severe cerebral damage followed neonatal meningitis. Accepted that damage flowed from the negligence: it was a case of 'wrongful birth' and costs attributable to the disability were recoverable. The report is followed by a useful commentary analysing the implications of cases decided since *McFarlane*. See also *Parkinson v St James & Seacroft University Hospital NHS Trust [2001]61 BMLR 100.*

5. **Rees v Darlington Memorial NHS Trust [2002] Lloyd's Rep Med 163.**
Birth of healthy child after negligent sterilisation. Mother with severe visual handicap entitled to claim extra costs of rearing the child that could be attributed to her disability.

6. **Greenfield v Flather and Ors [2001] Lloyd's Rep Med 143.**
Late diagnosis of unwanted pregnancy during contraceptive treatment. Mother, electing to give up her employment to look after the healthy child, claimed damages for economic loss and also that her right under Article 8 of the European Convention on Human Rights had been infringed (respect for private and family life). Both aspects of the claim were rejected by the Court of Appeal.

7. **Pearman v North Essex Health Authority [2000] Lloyd's Rep Med 174.**
Cauda Equina syndrome after unacceptable delay in microdiscectomy for prolapsed intervertebral disc. Defendant adduced evidence to show that the timing of surgical intervention did not affect outcome, despite conventional practice to intervene as soon as possible after the onset of urinary retention.

8. **Holtby v Brigham & Cowan (Hull) Ltd [2000] Lloyd's Rep Med 241.**
Claimant suffering from asbestosis was exposed during employment by the defendant and by other agencies. Claim brought solely against the defendant succeeded but damages were discounted to allow for contribution to his disease by other periods of employment. The injury was 'not indivisible'.

9. **Bonnington Castings Ltd v Wardlaw [1956] AC 613.**
Silicosis attributable to *both* negligent and non-negligent exposure to dust. Negligence made a material contribution and, although unable to demonstrate there would have been no injury but for the negligence, claimant succeeded.

10. **Fairchild v Glenhaven Funeral Services [2002] Lloyd's Rep Med 361.**
Successful appeal. Claim brought by executrix of estate of deceased who developed lung cancer after exposure to asbestos while working for a variety of employers. Even if the carcinoma had been induced by a single fibre, it was not necessary to prove which of many exposures was responsible.

11. **Beverley Pidgeon v Doncaster Health Authority [2002] Lloyd's Rep Med 130.**
Negligent failure correctly to identify an abnormal cervical smear was followed by a prolonged period without follow-up because the claimant repeatedly failed to heed medical advice that further checks were due, despite acknowledging she understood the importance of the test. A successful claim was brought after she developed invasive cervical cancer, but damages were reduced by two-thirds for her contributory negligence.

12. **Hotson v East Berks AHA [1987] AC 750.**
Delayed diagnosis of slipped epiphysis. Award of damages in proportion to magnitude of lost chance of a good outcome was reversed on appeal because an adverse outcome was already more likely than not.

13. **Judge v Huntingdon HA [1995] 6 Med LR 223.**
Negligent delay in diagnosis of breast cancer resulted in loss of an 80% chance of cure. *Quantification of the loss* was calculated on this basis. This contrasts with the 'all or nothing' approach to causation (see 12).

14. **Smith v National Health Service Litigation Authority [2001] Lloyd's Rep Med 90.**
Delayed diagnosis of congenital dislocation of the hip. The claim failed because breach of duty was not established but the judge accepted in principle that loss of the chance of a better medical outcome could found a valid claim. Although criticised, this judgement was applied in the negotiated settlement of cases arising from a negligent breast screening programme – see *Spink A.*

Causation and quantum: the legal issues. Clinical Risk 2001 7:219–223. Part 3 of a series on resolution of East Devon Breast Screening claims.

15. Joyce v Merton, Sutton & Wandsworth HA [1996] 7 Med LR 1.

    Allegedly negligent failure to consult a vascular surgeon when a weak pulse and cool limb followed brachial arteriotomy. The Bolam test is to be applied to determine what constitutes proper care.

16. Bolitho v City & Hackney HA [1998] AC 232 and [1998] Lloyd's Rep Med 26.

    House of Lords confirmed tests to be applied to determine consequence of a failure to act: what *would* the practitioner have done and what *should* the practitioner have done.

17. Wilsher v Essex AHA [1988] AC 1074.

    Retinopathy of prematurity occurred after negligent exposure to high concentrations of oxygen. Plaintiff failed to establish that oxygen toxicity, as distinct from other possible causes, was responsible in part or at all.

18. Ratcliffe v Plymouth & Torbay HA *et al* [1998] Lloyd's Rep Med 162.

    Unexplained neurological defect after spinal anaesthesia. Court satisfied on balance of probabilities that proper care had been exercised, even though no satisfactory explanation for injury was offered. Plea of *res ipsa loquitur* failed.

▶4

Financial considerations: compensation and costs

The outcome of a successful claim in negligence is an award of damages, a payment made to compensate the claimant for the injury caused and its consequences. The intention is to restore the claimant, so far as money is able, to the position he would have been in but for the negligent act. The size of the award bears no relationship to the perceived or actual magnitude of the alleged wrong-doing although very occasionally an award is enhanced to reflect injury to the claimant's feelings or pride, or because of the defendant's unacceptable behaviour[1]. Punitive or 'aggravated damages' are deemed inappropriate in claims for negligence because of conflict with the principle of compensation, but have been awarded for the tort of trespass to the person[2]. By contrast, damages for negligence in the United States *can* include a punitive element as well as compensation.

General damages

This is the sum awarded for pain, suffering and loss of amenity attributable to the injury. Figures are based upon Judicial Studies Board Guidelines which are updated regularly and which set a range within which awards for a particular injury are selected. Caselaw is used to establish or refute a particular point within any guideline range. This permits reasonable parity of awards for like injuries but also allows for differences in the impact on individuals of the same injury, for example a facial scar. The scale of general damages for claims valued at more than £10,000 was increased in March 2000[3] after the Law Commission reported that general damages in England and Wales were too low by comparison with other jurisdictions.

Interest is awarded on general damages at 2% from the date on which proceedings were served to the date of trial. The low rate reflects the regular updating of recommendations for general damages, the award for an individual being selected from figures current at the date of trial.

Special damages

These are losses specific to the individual which are attributable to the negligently caused injury. Past losses such as interruption of earnings, care and travel costs can be calculated reasonably accurately whereas future losses are hypothetical. However, even past losses are difficult to determine if there has been long delay between injury and trial, or detailed records have not been kept – for example by the self-employed.

Interest on past losses is recoverable from the date of injury to the date of trial and is awarded at half the 'appropriate rate' allowed on the High Court Special Investment Account over that period. The halving is because some of the past losses would have been incurred soon after the injury whereas others are still ongoing at the time of trial. Interest on the statutory bereavement award and funeral expenses, which are recoverable after a fatal accident, is awarded at the full appropriate rate from date of death to date of trial.

The concept of multiplier and multiplicand

Serious injury can have repercussions for an individual and his family which persist throughout and beyond his lifetime. The totality of the loss is determined at the time of trial or settlement and this entire sum is then available, either directly to the adult claimant of sound mind, or within the safe-keeping of the court for the benefit of minors and those of unsound mind. This 'accelerated receipt' means the claimant has the immediate benefit of funds which, but for the injury, would have taken a lifetime to acquire (earn) or to require (care costs). Invested wisely, these funds generate additional income and the capital increases in value to keep pace with inflation. An allowance must therefore be made to offset these benefits. Unpredictable variables and uncertainties for the individual must also be acknowledged when calculating, at any one time, what losses or needs may arise in the future. For this reason the legal process has developed the concept of *multiplier* and *multiplicand*.

The *multiplicand* is the annual net value of each element of future loss or expense, based on figures current at the date of trial.

The *multiplier* is the number of years over which the loss or expense is expected to occur, offset to allow for accelerated receipt and the uncertainties of predicting an individual's future.

Tables of multipliers have been constructed to reflect the rate of return on investments. Traditionally the figure was 4.5% but, in 1999, the House of Lords deemed the greater security of index-linked government stock was more appropriate[4]. A 3% return was applied thereafter and has since been reduced to 2.5%. The financial consequences are enormous. For example, the multiplier for a male claimant aged 20 at the time of trial and with a normal life expectancy (say 55 years) increases from 20.62 if the rate of return on investments is 4.5%, to 27.4 at 3% and 30.54 at 2.5%. In the context of actions arising within the National Health Service there is an obvious conflict between the need properly to compensate an individual harmed by negligently delivered medical treatment and the requirement to ensure that limited resources are used to provide high quality care to all. More broadly, the conflict lies between adequate compensation for the individual and the cost of insurance for the majority.

Provisional damages

The consequences of injury are not always immediately apparent. Some allowance for future deterioration may be made by including an additional sum to reflect the magnitude and significance of the risk (eg epilepsy after head injury). Alternatively provisional damages can be awarded at trial *provided* there is a real (ie admitted or proven) chance that at some future date the claimant will, as a result of the negligent act, develop some serious disease or suffer some serious deterioration in his physical or mental condition. This allows initial compensation only for the existing injury, coupled with a right, fixed by the court for a specified period, to claim further recompense if the predicted adverse future development does indeed occur.

Some specific elements of loss

Some heads of claim are easy to identify such as loss of earnings, pension rights or a requirement for new or adapted housing to accommodate the needs of a disabled person. High earning claimants secure far higher awards than those with low or no income because, without the negligent injury, they and their families would have enjoyed the benefits of the higher income. The purpose of the award is to compensate them for their loss. The apparent injustice of 'to he that hath shall more be given' is illusory because the award is not based on some generally applicable notional income but on the previous situation and potential of the individual.

If there is no measurable and predictable earnings loss, a claim may be allowed for compromise on the labour market (a *Smith v Manchester* award). This may also be appropriate for a young child whose career options are indeterminate. Alternatively the future losses of children are estimated from national average earnings in careers comparable to those of their parents or siblings. Such awards are never high because there is a large element of accelerated receipt and the loss is of a chance, not of a defined achievement.

Fatal accidents give rise to claims on behalf of the estate of the deceased (Law Reform (Miscellaneous Provisions) Act 1934) and those dependent on the deceased at the time of death (Fatal Accidents Act 1976). The calculation of special damages is particularly difficult because losses before trial, as well as those in the future, are hypothetical. In addition to any proven individual losses, close relatives (spouses and parents of children less than 18 years) are entitled to a statutory bereavement award, currently £10,000. However, such an award is not triggered by a still-born child, even if the still-birth was the consequence of negligence.

Possible future developments

The magnitude of an award of damages – quantum – is often as contentious as the legal basis for the claim. Some cases go to trial solely on this issue, even when liability has been determined or admitted[5]. Even in cases resolved by negotiation, there is often a very striking difference between the value of the claim as first calculated by the opposing legal teams. Sometimes this reflects a difference of medical opinion on future life expectancy but usually also includes major differences in the assessment of individual loss, need and the cost of providing for it. Here too expert opinion is obtained from diverse care therapists, employment experts and forensic accountants. Much time, effort and legal expense are then invested in resolving the differences.

Several changes have been proposed to reduce this conflict. One is the use of a single expert to advise on matters of quantum, either jointly instructed by defendants and claimants, or appointed by the court. A second is the development of guidelines for the care consequences and costs of specific injuries. A third possibility is the definition and compensation of immediate need with the provision thereafter of an annuity to cover need for the duration of the claimant's lifetime, thus avoiding calculations based upon tenuous assessments of prognosis for conditions where standards and outcome of medical care are changing rapidly. A further controversial proposal is the abolition of the statutory provision[6] which permits the costs of future medical treatment to be obtained privately without reference to availability on the NHS[7]. Inevitably there are protagonists and antagonists for all these developments and maintenance of the *status quo* is unlikely.

Funding Litigation

Litigation is costly. Claims in clinical negligence are among the most expensive, not least because expert evidence is so often required on all three aspects – breach of duty, causation of injury and quantum. It is common for costs to exceed the value of the claim when damages are less than £10,000. A significant proportion of these costs is incurred before it is possible to predict with any accuracy whether or not the claimant has reasonable prospects of success. If initial investigation suggests there are no grounds for further pursuit, the expenditure has all been in vain. If the prospects for success are equivocal, the claimant is tempted to continue but is then at risk of an adverse outcome at trial. A successful defendant can recoup the expense of defending the claim from an unsuccessful claimant who, if privately funded, is then responsible for the expenses incurred by both parties. Few patients are prepared to take such risks privately.

Legal Aid

Legal Aid was introduced in 1949 to assist those otherwise unable to afford legal advice, assistance or representation. It is means tested, those with some resources being required to contribute on a regular basis as the claim evolves. Children can obtain Legal Aid in their own name without reference to the resources of their parents. Since April 2000, Legal Aid has not been available for most personal injury and fatal accident claims but actions arising from clinical negligence are excepted. However, such claims can only be handled by solicitors holding a clinical negligence franchise awarded, monitored and renewed by the Legal Services Commission (LSC), and eligibility criteria for financial assistance are now more stringent. These measures are intended to weed out cases unlikely to succeed or where costs are disproportionate to value.

If a legally-aided action is lost, contributions made by the individual cannot be recovered and the Community Legal Services Fund suffers a loss. Conversely, the successful claimant can expect to recoup costs from the defendant sufficient to reimburse expenditure by the LSC and most if not all his own contribution. As a general rule however, a successful defendant cannot recover costs from a legally-aided party. These rules put the legally-aided claimant in a very strong financial position for as long as Legal Aid is continued. The defendant is bound to suffer financially – by paying both sides' costs if the defence fails or at least his own costs if successful. This creates a powerful incentive to settle out-of-court and so avoid the expense of trial. The grant of Legal Aid is subject to review as the case proceeds and will be withdrawn unless the LSC is satisfied further pursuit is likely to be cost-effective. Despite this requirement the perception among defendants is still of limitless support for claims without merit.

Conditional fee agreements

A conditional fee agreement (CFA) permits solicitors and counsel to enter into a contract with the claimant which provides for fees to be paid only if the case succeeds. A percentage uplift ('success fee') of up to 100% of the basic fee can also be charged in successful cases. The claimant's costs and success fee can be recovered by a successful claimant, as can the premium for any insurance arranged to cover possible liability for the costs of a successful defendant. The unsuccessful claimant will sacrifice any insurance premium, and the unsuccessful legal team will remain unpaid. The claimant's lawyers however are *not* responsible for the costs of a successful defendant, even if the litigant has pursued the claim under a CFA without insurance cover[8]. Insurance is not an obligatory element of a CFA, a number of claimants obtain after-the-event insurance, and some are insured for legal expenses in any event through household or other insurance policies. An anticipated benefit of CFAs is a reduction in prolonged, unwarranted legal advice to pursue unmeritorious claims.

Funding the defence of clinical negligence claims

The escalating volume and value of claims for medical negligence during the 1980s led to a rapid rise in premiums for professional indemnity, a problem resolved for practitioners employed within NHS hospitals by the advent of NHS indemnity in 1990[9]. However, this provides *only* for claims arising from events occurring within the course of the practitioner's employment.

The role of the *medical defence organisations (MDOs)* has changed as a result. While continuing to provide support and assistance to their members, they no longer have financial responsibility for actions brought against trusts and have no control over the conduct of the litigation. At present they retain both control and financial responsibility for actions arising from private practice and those brought against insured general practitioners and overseas members. The advent of Primary Care Trusts, which have a duty to ensure good clinical governance, raises the possibility that claims arising in primary care may also be covered by NHS indemnity in the future.

The **Clinical Negligence Scheme for Trusts (CNST)** was introduced in April 1995 to pool the cost of successful claims against NHS hospital trusts. Claims in excess of £10,000 arising before April 1995 were covered by an **Existing Liabilities Scheme (ELS),** provided certain management criteria were fulfilled. Membership of the CNST is now compulsory. Premiums are determined according to the nature and volume of clinical work, and adjusted according to the standard of each trust's clinical risk management arrangements as judged against established criteria.

The **National Health Service Litigation Authority** (NHSLA), established in 1995 as a special health authority, is responsible for handling all NHS clinical negligence and employment-related claims against NHS trusts, and for the administration and supervision of the CNST. A separate 'small claims unit' was set up recently to handle claims valued below £25,000. Trusts no longer need to set aside revenue for clinical litigation other than the CNST premium. The Authority also has a remit to sustain or improve patient care, to ensure that patients have access to appropriate remedies and recompense, and that claims handling is carried out consistently, efficiently and cost-effectively[10]. Centralised management should also facilitate the compilation of accurate data for the number, nature and cost of clinical claims.

References

1. Kralj v McGrath [1986] 1 All ER 54.
   Attempted cephalic version of a second twin without general anaesthesia. Aggravated damages deemed wholly inappropriate in action brought in negligence and breach of contract. Compensatory damages to be increased instead.
2. Appleton and Others v Garrett [1997] 8 Med LR 75.
   Dentist carried out unnecessary treatment for financial gain. Award for the tort of trespass to the person included aggravated damages assessed at 15% of the figure for general damages.
3. Heil v Rankin and Another and other appeals [2000] Lloyd's Rep Med 203.
   One of 8 test cases, 3 derived from actions in clinical negligence, heard together by the Court of Appeal. General damages should not be increased for awards below £10,000 but above this threshold there should be a tapered increase to a maximum of one third in awards for the most catastrophic injuries.
4. Wells v Wells [1999] 1 AC 345.
   House of Lords decision establishing 3% as the guideline discount rate for calculating future losses. The rate has since been reduced to 2.5%.

5. Ruff v The Royal Victoria Infirmary and Associated Hospitals NHS Trust [2001] Lloyd's Rep Med 530.
   Severe cerebral damage following a hypoxic incident in infancy. Negligence was admitted and general damages, some special damages, and the multiplicand for future losses were all agreed. Trial solely on life expectancy and how it should be determined. A clinical rather than statistical approach was preferred.

6. Law Reform (Personal Injuries) Act 1948 s2(4).
   In calculating medical expenses, the possibility of using facilities under the NHS Acts is to be disregarded.

7. Parkhouse v North Devon Healthcare Trust [2002] Lloyd's Rep Med 100.
   Damages for severely disabled child which *were* discounted to allow for equipment provided by State services. Claim for a contingency fund for future technical aids was dismissed as too speculative, despite agreement by both experts.

8. Hodgson v Imperial Tobacco Ltd [1998] 2 All ER 673.
   Court of Appeal ruling that lawyers acting under conditional fee arrangements on behalf of unsuccessful, uninsured claimants are not responsible for the costs of the successful defendant.

9. Claims of medical negligence against NHS hospital and community doctors and dentists. Department of Health Circular: HC 89(34).
   Health Circular published in 1989 setting out arrangement for NHS indemnity to apply from January 1st 1990. Authorities could no longer *require* staff to subscribe to a recognised professional defence organisation but should encourage staff to ensure they have 'adequate defence cover as appropriate'.

10. The National Health Service Litigation Authority Framework Document. Department of Health, September 1996.
    Sets out aims, objectives and functions of the NHSLA and how it relates to ministers and the NHS Executive.

►5
Legal procedure; the Woolf reforms; role of expert witnesses

New civil procedure rules came into force in April 1999, based on Lord Woolf's report into civil justice[1]. They introduced radical reform intended to achieve just results expeditiously, with proportionality between the cost and value of claims. Control of the conduct of cases is now vested in the courts, the rules operate in both County and High Court actions, and simplified terminology applies throughout.

Choice of court

Claims for personal injury, including clinical negligence, are started in the County Court if valued at less than £50,000. Claims of higher value can be started in either the County Court or the High Court. Many, but not all, clinical negligence claims valued at more than £50,000 are started in the High Court because value, complexity or general importance are deemed to warrant the deliberations of a High Court Judge. Designated clinical negligence trial centres with judges specifically trained and experienced in medical law are planned as part of the Woolf reforms.

Appeals from final orders are heard by three Lord Justices in the Court of Appeal. Leave to appeal is never granted lightly and, unless an issue of principle is at stake, the burden is on the appellant to show that the judge at first instance has erred. Challenges to law or principle will be explored more readily than fact or discretion which are only rarely overturned. This is because the judge at first instance has the benefit of taking evidence directly from the witnesses, whereas the Court of Appeal deals solely with the transcript.

Final appeals reach the House of Lords and require leave, either from the Court of Appeal or House of Lords itself. Matters of exceptional significance are heard by a court of five or even seven Law Lords, lesser matters being dealt with by three. Appeal to the House of Lords arising from claims in clinical negligence claims is infrequent, used most often to clarify an important principle or determine legal policy on controversial ethical issues[2,3].

Clinical Negligence Pre-Action Protocol

A prescribed pre-action procedure is now mandatory for claims in both personal injury and clinical negligence. Its purpose is to resolve as many disputes as possible without formal litigation and, in the context of clinical negligence, to maintain or restore the relationship between patient and health care provider. These objectives are to be met by early investigation and appraisal of merit, and a reciprocal willingness to share expert evidence.

The clinical negligence pre-action protocol consists of three essential steps:

▶ disclosure of medical records

▶ letter of claim

▶ response to the letter of claim.

Disclosure of medical records

A request for records should provide sufficient information to alert the trust or practitioner to the nature and magnitude of the adverse outcome and specify, as far as possible, which records are required. Use of a standard form is recommended. Copy records should be provided within 40 days of the request, and explanation offered promptly if there are genuine reasons why this target cannot be met. Disclosure should be voluntary – it can in any case be enforced by the courts or sought by the patient under the terms of the Data Protection Act 1998. Disclosure of sensitive additional information such as internal audit reports is considered in chapter 6.

The Letter of Claim

This letter is based upon initial expert opinion obtained to assess whether the claimant has grounds for seeking redress. Prepared by the claimant's legal advisers, it sets out the basis for the claim in formal but non-legalistic terms. It should include

▶ a summary of the facts, with a chronology if appropriate

▶ the allegations of breach of duty

▶ the harm which is alleged to have been caused as a result

▶ an indication of the value of the claim.

The claimant (ie his legal advisers) may elect to disclose expert evidence at this stage and is expected to do so if combining the letter of claim with an offer to settle (see below).

A letter of claim is not deemed to be legally binding and, if the matter proceeds to litigation, discrepancies may be detected in subsequent pleadings. Similarly the assessment of financial loss may be no more than preliminary, particularly in complex, high-value claims.

Response to the letter of claim

The letter of claim should be acknowledged within 14 days of receipt and should name the individual responsible for handling subsequent correspondence. The letter of response should follow within three months from the date of the letter of claim and should set out

- what, if any, part of the claim is admitted

- what allegations are denied

- reasoned argument for the denial

- factual commentary or chronology if the claimant's version is disputed.

The defendant should respond to any offer to settle, giving reasons for the stance adopted. A counter-offer can be made, with expert evidence adduced in support. Evidence refuting liability can also usefully be disclosed – for example, opinion, protocols or guidelines to rebut allegations of breach of duty, or expert evidence to deny causation of injury.

Resolution without legal proceedings

The steps outlined above suffice to permit negotiated settlement of a significant proportion of claims. If there is a risk that the claimant's position may be compromised by delay since the allegedly negligent event (see section below on limitation), formal legal action may be commenced by the issue but not service of proceedings. Alternatively the defendant can agree informally to waive limitation for a specified period. Some latitude on the timing of letters of response has crept into practice, but carries the potential for cost sanctions imposed by the court if the matter cannot be resolved without formal litigation.

Legal Proceedings

The formal start is the 'issue' of proceedings. A claim form (formerly a writ or summons) and fee are submitted to the court which then registers the claim, allocates a unique case number and date-stamps the form. It is preferable but not mandatory for particulars of claim to be prepared at the same time. The claim form must be 'served' (ie delivered to, by a legally acceptable route) on the defendant or his legal representative (eg hospital legal department or solicitors acting for a medical defence organisation) within four months of issue. In practical terms, the particulars of claim are more important than the claim form because they set out the factual basis for the claim, the allegations of breach of duty and of consequent injury. A medical report substantiating the injury and its consequences ('condition and prognosis report') should be served at the same time as the particulars, together with a schedule of special damages (see chapter 4). The claim form, particulars and report should each incorporate a statement of truth. This is a declaration that the party submitting the document believes the facts stated in it are true; a false declaration, made without honest belief in its truth, amounts to contempt of court. Although the claimant's solicitor often makes the declaration on both claim form and particulars, the attestation is to the *claimant's* belief in the factual veracity of the document.

Defending a claim

It is incumbent upon a defendant either to file an admission, prepare and serve a defence, or file an acknowledgment of service within 14 days of service of the particulars of claim. Provided service has been acknowledged within 14 days, the defendant has up to 28 days from service of the particulars of claim in which to serve the defence. The parties can agree for this period to be extended for up to another 28 days. However, now that the courts rather than the parties have control over the pace of litigation, any agreement to extend the time for service of the defence must be notified to the court in writing.

The defence must state which facts and allegations are

▶ admitted

▶ denied

▶ not admitted – ie require to be proved.

Allegations not specifically answered in one of these three ways are deemed to be admitted.

Limitation is a procedural device for denying liability when the claim has been brought out of time. The Limitation Act 1980 requires that actions for personal injury must be started either

▸ within three years from the date of accrual of the cause of action (ie the negligent event)

▸ or within three years of the date of knowledge.

Claims arising from death must be brought within three years of the date of death or three years from the date the claimant or representative first had knowledge.

Date of knowledge is defined as the date on which the claimant first knew or should reasonably have known

▸ the identity of the defendant *and*

▸ that the injury was significant *and*

▸ was attributable in whole or in part to the act or omission alleged to be negligent.

Knowledge that the defendant's conduct *is* actionable, as a matter of law, is not required.

The three-year period does not operate against persons 'under a disability'. The term refers to children below 18 years, and those of unsound mind, sometimes referred to as 'patients'. A person is of unsound mind if, by reason of a mental disorder within the meaning of the Mental Health Act 1983, he is incapable of managing and administering his property and affairs. The three-year period begins to run against a youthful claimant when he reaches 18 years. Those of unsound mind either at the time of the incident or as a result of it, are not subject to limitation unless they recover their faculties. The Act also provides a discretionary power which can allow the action to continue, despite a prolonged lapse of time. Trial of limitation as a preliminary point may then be needed, either before, or at the start of, the trial of the action. Amendments to the Limitation Act 1980 are anticipated to secure greater uniformity and define a time-limit, even for actions brought on behalf of those under a disability. The impact on actions in clinical negligence may be limited because although discretion to disapply limitation will not be available in general, it is to be retained in the context of personal injury.

The new procedural rules require the defence to include *reasons* for denying facts or allegations. Formerly a 'holding defence' was acceptable – a legal device to avoid comment on the detail of the claim. Perceived by patients as denial by the *doctor*, not merely part of legal manoeuvring, the holding defence added a sense of insult to injury. Now the defendant must offer explanation for what occurred, including if necessary rebuttal of the claimant's medical report or schedule. It too must now include a statement of truth by or on behalf of the practitioner or trust.

Further legal exchanges may then follow between the parties – formulation of a reply to the defence, or a request for further information (further and better particulars) or specific questions (interrogatories) directed to identified individuals. The totality of this formal documentation constitutes the statement of case (pleadings).

Subsequent conduct

Once the defence has been filed (ie received by the court), the parties are required to co-operate with the court to ensure proper allocation to a particular legal 'track'. There are small claims, fast and multi-track options, each with its own arrangements for staging and timing. Clinical negligence claims are usually allocated to the multi-track option which is reserved for matters considered complex. Thereafter the court sets a timetable for the exchange of witness statements (ie witnesses of fact – the claimant/patient and clinical staff involved in the incident), disclosure of documents, exchange of expert reports and, if necessary, a date for trial. Few clinical negligence claims reach court. Most are either settled by negotiation or discontinued by the claimant. The new rules permit either party to make an offer ('Part 36 offer') to settle on specific terms. Significant cost penalties are incurred if an offer is refused and the refusing party subsequently does less well at trial, a provision which provides a powerful incentive to make or accept carefully considered proposals.

A number of cases are settled without a formal admission of liability, although lay persons, particularly patient and practitioner, are likely to interpret such an outcome as tantamount to an admission. Economic expediency is also taken into consideration, particularly when the value of the claim is low by comparison with the costs of trial. There is good reason for this. The general rule is that a successful party recovers its costs from the losing party, but claimants assisted by Legal Aid (currently the majority) are an exception. Thus even a successful defence is costly for the NHS or medical defence organisation. There are obvious conflicts between competing requirements to conserve scarce financial resources and preserve the professional reputations of hospitals and practitioners by presenting a robust defence when appropriate, while at the same time ensuring that those wronged by clinical error are properly compensated. Claims in clinical negligence should not be perceived as an easy route to securing compensation, nor should practitioners feel that justice – or their reputation – are being sacrificed to economic expediency. A better view is to recognise that Legal Aid is rarely continued for cases which do not have at least an arguable chance of succeeding and that liability is often a matter of corporate rather than individual responsibility, in other words, a system error[4].

Alternative dispute resolution (ADR)

This is a generic term encompassing all methods for reaching settlement other than litigation.

Arbitration is rarely used in clinical claims. It is consensual in that issues are determined by a nominated or agreed arbitrator who is conversant with the subject of dispute. The conduct of the arbitration is adversarial, cases being presented by counsel and supported by expert evidence in a manner similar to trial. It is used most often in commercial disputes arising from contract.

Mediation is also a consensual procedure in which the parties must agree not only to proceed to mediation, but must also agree the terms of any settlement reached before they are bound by it. The mediator is usually recruited from a professional agency and, having been sent documents outlining the basis for the claim and its defence, convenes a meeting attended by both parties and their solicitors. In a common forum, both parties summarise the essential elements of their case and then they disperse, each party with advisers to a separate room. The mediator then enters discussions with each party in turn, exploring what their hopes and expectations are, what features are seen as essential elements of any settlement and what awareness each side has of weaknesses in its case. Knowledge acquired by the mediator is confidential unless permission is given to relay it to the other side. Unlike a litigated settlement, mediation can encompass elements of redress other than financial compensation – an apology, explanation, commitment to a particular course of action by the trust or on behalf of a named individual. The process is confidential, fosters co-operation, and has the potential to disperse emotion, re-establish confidence and restore easy communication between doctor and patient. Solutions cannot be imposed. The role of the mediator is purely to *assist the parties* to reach an agreed settlement.

The **NHS mediation pilot study**[5] sought to identify the potential for mediating claims in clinical negligence. Take-up was disappointingly low but cases which were mediated usually reached settlement and most participants expressed satisfaction. Reluctance to embark on mediation was apparent among both claimants and defendants – a finding echoed in the civil courts in general. Despite this disappointing result, mediation has been specifically recommended by a Commons Select Health Committee Report on adverse clinical incidents[6], has been rendered more attractive by changes in funding policy, and can be required by the courts, possibly even as a pre-requisite to the commencement of legal proceedings. It has been endorsed for claims in clinical negligence by both the audit commission and the NHSLA, but its potential may be limited by the number of cases now reaching early negotiated settlement solely on the basis of the pre-action protocol.

Other techniques of alternative dispute resolution such as early neutral evaluation or expert determination have not been explored in the context of claims arising from clinical practice.

The role of the expert witness

Professional opinion provides the basis for judicial determination of both breach of duty and causation of injury. A just legal outcome requires that opinion to be accurate, up to date, comprehensive, objective and non-partisan. Such ideals have not always been realised. The new procedural rules define the duties of experts, specify the content and format of reports and require that they are addressed to the court. The essential duty, to assist the court, must override any obligation to the party providing instructions. The report must include

- details of the expert's qualifications
- details of learned literature on which he has relied in formulating his opinion
- the substance of all material instructions provided to him
- details of persons assisting with tests carried out and whether they were supervised
- clarification of which facts are within the expert's own knowledge
- a summary of the *range* of medical opinion and reasons for the opinion held

▶ a summary of the conclusions reached, with any necessary qualification

▶ a statement confirming that the expert understands his duty to the court, and that he has complied and will continue to comply with this duty.

The report must also be verified by a statement of truth confirming the opinion as true and complete, and that facts within the expert's knowledge are identified and believed to be true.

The courts have been given far greater power over expert evidence. It may not be adduced without leave, and oral testimony in particular is restricted to what is reasonably required to resolve the proceedings. Thus the court can limit the number of experts, direct that evidence on an issue be given by a single expert and, if the parties cannot agree on a nominee, can select the expert or appoint an assessor to assist. The court can, and often does, direct that there be a meeting of experts requiring them to identify the essential issues and if possible, agree some or all of them. Alternatively the court can specify which issues are to be discussed and require the experts to prepare a joint statement setting out any matters on which they agree, those on which they disagree and why. Written questions to the opposing expert are also permitted. Inevitably these powers have spawned conflict[7-9] because of concerns that authoritative experts can overrule more timid colleagues, that decision-making has been handed back to the medical profession, and that reliance on single experts may be inappropriate. Despite these misgivings, meetings of experts have been welcomed and are usually considered helpful. Conflict is minimised by careful construction of the agenda, preferably with medical input, and using as far as possible questions which require only a 'yes' or 'no' answer. Parties are not legally bound by an agreement reached by experts unless they agree to be bound, and the court retains the power to act as final arbiter. Some commentators argue for the presence of both parties' legal advisers at meetings of experts whereas others consider more fruitful discussion will take place in their absence. This conflict of opinion has yet to be resolved.

References

1. Access to Justice. Final report by The Right Honourable the Lord Woolf MR to the Lord Chancellor on the civil justice system in England and Wales. HMSO, July 1996.
   Actions in medical negligence singled out as the area where civil justice failed most conspicuously. Reasons included disproportion between costs and damages, particularly in low value cases, a low rate of success, excessive delay, prolonged unwarranted pursuit of unmeritorious claims or indefensible defences, and more intense suspicion and lack of co-operation between the parties than in many other areas of litigation. A damning commentary!

2. Gillick v W Norfolk & Wisbech AHA [1986] AC 112.

   An issue of social principle: is it acceptable to provide contraceptive advice to a child below 16 years without parental consent? Decision of the House of Lords forms the basis for defining the consensual capacity of children.

3. Airedale NHS Trust v Bland [1993] 4 Med LR 39.

   Validity of withdrawing life-sustaining treatment from a patient in persistent vegetative state. The House of Lords was careful to point out that each case should be considered individually – policy was a matter for parliament.

4. Reason J. Human error: models and management. BMJ 2000 320: 768–70.

   Psychologist's account of the sources of human error – the person approach and the system approach.

5. Mulcahy L. Mediating Medical Negligence Claims: an option for the future? HMSO, January 2000.

   Final report on the NHS mediation pilot study.

6. Sixth Report of the House of Commons Select Committee: Procedures related to adverse clinical incidents and outcomes in medical care. HMSO, November 1999.

   At paragraph 130, the Committee recommends 'that the Government reviews, clarifies and improves the funding, and other, arrangements relating to mediation and acts on the findings of the pilot mediation scheme.'

7. Oxley v Penwarden [2001] Lloyd's Rep Med 347.

   Peripheral arterial disease leading to amputation. Successful appeal against an order to instruct a single 'causation' expert or accept one appointed by the court. See also *Sims v Birmingham Health Authority [2001] Lloyd's Rep Med 382* where a similar conclusion was reached.

8. Hubbard and Ors v Lambeth, Southwark and Lewisham Health Authority and Ors [2002] Lloyd's Rep Med 8.

   Court ordered meeting of experts not precluded by sensitivity of those who had criticised a pre-eminent colleague in written reports which had already been exchanged.

9. Peet v Mid-Kent Healthcare NHS Trust [2002] Lloyd/s Rep Med 33.

   Court directed joint instruction of non-medical quantum experts; claimant sought to confer with them in the absence of the defendants. Such a meeting was opposed by the defendants and rejected by the court as inconsistent with CPR. The desirability of single quantum experts was reiterated.

   The report is followed by a useful commentary from three experienced clinical negligence counsel on the practical implications of instructing single experts, particularly in high-value claims.

▶6

Confidentiality and disclosure

Growing public concern about the unnecessary recording, retention or dissemination of personal details has led to new legislation and recommendations which seek to resolve conflict between the rights of individuals to privacy and preservation of confidentiality, and the needs of society for disclosure of relevant information. In 1997, the Caldicott Committee reported variable compliance with good practice and recommended the appointment of Organisation Guardians to improve the security and confidentiality of clinical information. HSC 99(012) sets out the requirements for all trusts to appoint a Caldicott Guardian whose responsibilities include the supervision of local protocols governing the handling of patient-identifiable information and its disclosure across organisational boundaries. New legislation has also defined more clearly patients' rights and practitioners' responsibilities.

Statutory provisions

The *Data Protection Act 1998* came into force in March 2000. It imposes duties on data controllers and processors and provides patients with

▶ rights of access to manual and electronic records, subject to specific exceptions

▶ rights of verification and correction.

Rights of access to the records of deceased persons are afforded to personal representatives and those who may have a claim arising from the death by the *Access to Health Records Act 1990*. The *Human Rights Act 1998* includes a right to freedom of expression (Article 10) and confirms a responsibility to prevent disclosure of information imparted in confidence. Article 8 defines a right to respect for private and family life, home and correspondence but includes exceptions based on public need. The *Access to Medical Reports Act 1988* provides a right to patients to inspect or be supplied with a copy of medical reports prepared about them for employ-ment or insurance purposes by a practitioner *who is or has been responsible for their clinical care.* Reports prepared by an independent practitioner who has never adopted a therapeutic relationship with the patient are not covered by either the Data Protection Act 1998 or the Access to Medical Reports Act of 1988. The *Freedom of Information Act 2000* provides only for access to non-personal information held by public authorities, for example policies for the provision of services.

Disclosure of medical records

Health Records are defined in the Data Protection Act 1998 as any record which consists of

► information relating to the physical or mental health or condition of an individual

► and has been made by or on behalf of a health professional in connection with the care of that individual.

The term 'any record' includes paper-based records, and information held electronically in the form of microfiche, optical disks, x-ray films, video-tapes, compact disks, photographs or photographic slides.

Care, as defined in the Access to Medical Reports Act 1988, includes examination, investigation or diagnosis for the purposes of any form of medical treatment. Documentation which does not lie within these defini-tions should be filed separately to lessen the risk of unauthorised disclosure if there is a request for 'the medical notes'.

The general rule is that confidential information must not be released to any third party without the consent of the patient. This rule can be waived if disclosure is required by statute (eg notifiable diseases), or where the safety of the public or an identified individual is at risk[1]. Many of the exceptions are a matter of professional discretion rather than of law[2], the guiding principle being that the practitioner must be able to give good reason for disclosure.

There are a number of exceptions to the right to disclosure under the Data Protection and Access to Health Records Acts, most importantly

► if the health professional believes disclosure is likely to cause serious harm to the physical or mental health of the patient or any other person

► if the information relates to, or has been provided by, an identifiable third party who has not consented to disclosure

▶ if, in the context of deceased persons, there is written evidence that disclosure would be contrary to the wishes of the deceased.

Disclosure in the context of litigation

Voluntary disclosure of case notes to a patient's solicitor requires the written consent of the patient or representative. This is so whether the records sought are the property of a potential defendant or an uninvolved practitioner or trust. The claimant's express authority is *not* required for disclosure to the trust or practitioner's legal advisers when a patient intimates an intention to take action against them. Either confidentiality is deemed to have been waived or it can be argued that disclosure is in the public interest to ensure prompt, efficient and just disposal of the case.

Compulsory disclosure can be enforced by court order against a potential defendant before an action begins, or against an uninvolved third party after proceedings have commenced. Practitioners can also be summoned to attend court, either to give oral evidence of matters within their knowledge or to produce documentation within their control. They are obliged to attend and only exceptionally might a judge exercise discretion and disallow sensitive questioning.

The potential litigant can now access health records most easily under the terms of the relevant legislation but the extent of disclosure may be more restricted than can be ordered by the court on individual application. For example, an audit report affecting an individual is not part of the 'health record' but could be sought by application to the court for specific discovery. Disclosure of medical and nursing notes is now usually made without question and most disputes centre on the release of records of patients with mental illness[3]. Claims for compensation arising from alleged breach of confidentiality[4] are rare because such a claim can only succeed if

▶ the information has the necessary quality of confidence

▶ has been imparted in circumstances importing an obligation of confidence

▶ unauthorised use of the information has caused detriment to the party imparting it.

The Data Protection Act 1998 makes statutory provision for compensation if a data processor contravenes the terms of the Act but here too the claimant must prove that damage resulted.

Disclosure in specific circumstances

Loss or destruction of records – including X-rays and charts – is likely to be interpreted to the disadvantage of the record-holder, even if wholly innocent. This is particularly so if records are destroyed when it is already clear that legal proceedings are in contemplation[5].

Inquiries and internal audit reports often contain sensitive information and may identify errors of procedure or their implementation. Audit which identifies individual patients is 'confidential' and should be treated as such. The use of anonymised data is preferred if wider disclosure is required to prompt system changes. Reports prepared in contemplation of litigation are 'privileged' – in other words, immune from disclosure. However, litigation as the sole or prime purpose *at the time of preparation* is the cardinal requirement. A confidential accident report, prepared in accordance with an NHS Circular, dealt not only with possible litigation but also considered if action was needed to prevent repetition. Disclosure was ordered on the grounds that the second purpose was at least as important as the first[6]. In another case, privilege in a report prepared solely in contemplation of litigation was deemed to have been waived when it was disclosed to an expert who then made reference to it in his own report[7]. Alternatively the judge was prepared to exercise his discretion in favour of disclosure. There is no judicial *authority* for a duty of candour resting on professional staff in the context of actions in professional negligence, but the concept is widely and increasingly endorsed. Concerns that a finding of negligence is inevitable, if a report advocating system change after an adverse incident is disclosed, are unfounded. Negligence is determined by the standards which pertained at the time of the incident: being wise after the event is not necessarily indicative of poor practice.

The *results of research* can be published or disclosed without breach of confidentiality *provided* individual patients cannot be identified[8]. Disclosure of medical records to a public body can also be ordered if there is a sufficiently compelling public interest to do so and provided there are sufficient and adequate safeguards[9]. In cases of conflict, judicial input may be necessary. The *Health and Social Care Act 2001* permits the Secretary of State for Health to regulate the processing of patient information required in the public interest or in the interests of improving patient care. Subordinate legislation governing disclosure for the purposes of public health surveillance and the maintenance of cancer registries came into effect in June 2002.

Disclosure of medical records at or before an inquest is sometimes requested either by the coroner or by the relatives of the deceased. The

Access to Health Records Act 1990 provides for disclosure to a deceased's personal representative or any person who may have a claim arising from the patient's death. The court can also order disclosure of medical notes in favour of the same persons before an inquest but only for the sole purpose of ascertaining the cause of death[10]. It is doubtful if the coroner has a *power* to secure disclosure of notes before the inquest. However he is required to examine, on oath, all persons having knowledge as to the facts of the death whom he considers it expedient to examine, can issue a subpoena requiring attendance (with penalties for non-compliance) and can impose a fine upon a witness who, without lawful excuse, refuses to answer a question put to him. In view of these provisions, it is hardly surprising that voluntary disclosure of notes to both coroner and family is now usually given on request.

References

1. W v Egdell [1989] 2 WLR 689.
   Psychiatrist voluntarily disclosed to a mental hospital and the Home Office an unfavourable report on a paranoid schizophrenic, who had been convicted of manslaughter but was, by then, seeking less stringent detention. Public interest in disclosure outweighed W's private interests. In the US case of *Tarasoff v Regents of University of California*, it was held that a psychologist owed a duty of care to a particular woman, murdered by one of his patients who had expressed an intention to kill her. She should have been forewarned, despite breach of confidentiality.
2. Confidentiality: Protecting and Providing Information. Guidelines provided by the General Medical Council, 2000.
   Amplifies the recommendations of GMC's general guidance in *Good Medical Practice*.
3. R v Mid-Glamorgan FHSA *ex parte* Martin [1994] 5 Med LR 383.
   Schizophrenic patient sought disclosure of medical records antedating Access to Health Records Act. Court of Appeal held there was no common law right of access and claimant was excluded by the terms of the Act.
4. Cornelius v de Taranto [2001] All ER (D) 227 (Oct); EWCA Civ 1511.
   Forensic psychiatrist, concerned about the mental health of the claimant, sent a copy of a medico-legal report arising in the context of alleged unfair dismissal to the claimant's GP and a consultant psychiatrist without consent. The report was treated as part of the claimant's NHS 'medical records'. The claimant was awarded £3,000 for breach of confidentiality but a claim for defamation was dismissed on the basis of 'justification'.
5. Hammond v W Lancs HA [1998] Lloyd's Rep Med 146.
   X-rays destroyed, despite receipt of a letter before action, because hospital did not consider they were part of a patient's medical records, a view regarded by the judge as 'wholly unacceptable'.
6. Lask v Gloucester HA [1991] 2 Med LR 379.
   Accident report prepared after patient fell in hospital grounds. NHS Circular (55)66 identifies purpose as preparation for litigation *and* measures to prevent repetition. Disclosure of the accident report was ordered.
7. Clough v Tameside & Glossop HA [1998] Lloyd's Rep Med 69.
   Claim arising from birth of child with Down's syndrome after alleged failure to accede to a request for amniocentesis. Report prepared, at request of MDU, by an SHO involved in antenatal care was relayed to psychiatrist instructed on behalf of the hospital to provide expert comment on magnitude of plaintiff's psychiatric injury. Psychiatrist alluded to the SHO's report and, when psychiatric evidence was disclosed, plaintiff sought and obtained SHO's report.

8. R v Department of Health *ex parte* Source Informatics Ltd [2000] Lloyd's Rep Med 76.

   Court of Appeal decision permitting disclosure, for commercial purposes, of anonymised prescription data. Issue deemed to be of such importance that representation and intervention in the appeal were allowed on behalf of the GMC, MRC, ABPI and the National Pharmaceutical Association.

9. A Health Authority v X and Ors [2002] Lloyd's Rep Med 139.

   Health Authority sought disclosure of patient records to assist investigation of a possible breach of GP Terms of Service. Disclosure to a public body was deemed contrary to the Human Rights Act 1998 but can be (and was) authorised if there is a compelling public interest satisfying criteria of necessity and proportionality, and sufficient and adequate safeguards are available.

10. Stobart v Nottingham HA [1992] 3 Med LR 284.

    Discovery of medical records before an inquest deemed to lie within Supreme Court Rules for pre-action disclosure. Ascertainment or attempts to ascertain the cause of death ... not a collateral purpose but well within the reasons for granting discovery. However, any attempt to go beyond the one issue (ie cause of death) would not be permissible.

►7
Consent; minors and the mentally incapacitated; research; training

Intentional, non-consensual touching is a tort (battery) or, if carried out in anger, a criminal offence. Unlike actions founded in negligence, claims for battery do not need to prove that injury has occurred as a result – the mere fact of non-consensual touching is sufficient to establish liability. However, attempts to bring actions for battery claiming invalid consent to medical treatment rarely succeed[1], provided the claimant has consented in general terms[2]. Claims founded on alleged insufficiency of information rendering consent invalid are brought in negligence, not battery, and so proof of consequential injury is necessary if the claim is to succeed.

What constitutes valid consent?

Consent to treatment is only valid if the patient is

- ► competent to take the decision

- ► provided with sufficient information

- ► acts voluntarily.

Competence to take the decision[3] requires the ability to

- ► understand information given

- ► retain and believe it, and

- ► use it to reach a reasoned decision.

The nature of consent

Implied consent is the basis for many diagnostic or therapeutic interventions, eg physical examination or venepuncture. *Express written consent* is preferred for procedures which are more than minimally invasive, require general anaesthesia or are associated with significant risk. The fact that a consent form has been signed is evidence only that the patient has consented to the procedure, *not* proof that the consent is necessarily valid (eg adequately informed).

The **doctrine of necessity** is the basis for assuming consent when urgent, life-saving treatment is deemed necessary but the patient is unable to provide valid consent. It extends only to those measures which are required immediately. Non-urgent treatment which a practitioner considers advisable (ie in the patient's best interests), or more conveniently carried out at the same time, is not covered and, if performed, may prompt disciplinary proceedings and/or a claim for damages[4].

Was consent given voluntarily?

This is rarely a cause of conflict but has sufficed to persuade the court to authorise blood transfusion to a former Jehovah's witness whose written declaration against such treatment, made while still legally competent, was attributed to parental pressure[5]. However, there must be evidence that there *was* undue influence[6] and that it sufficed to overrule volition[7].

What constitutes 'sufficient information'?

Sufficiency of information is still defined at English law by the *Bolam* principle – judicial appraisal of professional opinion[8] – whereas in other jurisdictions the court determines what suffices[9]. However an increasingly prescriptive approach is being adopted in the English courts[10], a trend given greater momentum by concerns arising from paediatric cardiac surgery at Bristol Royal Infirmary and the non-consensual retention of tissues and organs after post mortem examination at the Royal Liverpool Children's Hospital[11]. Current recommendations[12,13] advocate more detailed disclosure than has been customary in the past, and revised consent forms provide better evidence that appropriate information has been relayed by a suitably experienced practitioner. Factors to consider when determining what constitutes 'appropriate' information should include both the magnitude of the possible adverse consequence and the likelihood that it will occur.

Claimants bringing an action founded on the allegation that consent was invalidated because the information given fell below an acceptable standard, must be able to show

▶ that the information given was, in fact, inadequate by accepted standards *and*

▶ consent would have been withheld had the proper information been supplied.

It can be difficult for the claimant to satisfy the court on the second limb of the test if the risk which materialised occurs infrequently and worthwhile benefit was anticipated from the treatment[14]. However, such actions have succeeded if the claimant can provide convincing testimony of the alternative policy which would have been adopted had sufficient information been given[15,16].

Who is entitled to consent or withhold consent to medical treatment?

Adult patients are assumed to be competent to consent to treatment in the absence of evidence to the contrary. They may withhold consent, even to life-saving treatment[5], and can do so by means of an 'advance directive' provided the decision was made when the patient was

▶ demonstrably competent

▶ acting voluntarily, and

▶ the decision covers the circumstances which prevail when treatment is contemplated.

Treatment initiated or continued in contravention of the clearly expressed wishes of a competent subject can found a claim for damages[17]. Assessing competence may require independent psychiatric advice if time and opportunity allow. There are no clear guidelines on the proper course of action if, during a procedure for which consent has been properly obtained, a patient requests that it be terminated. In a Canadian case[18] it was held that continued validity of consent was a matter for the exercise of medical judgment.

Consent by or on behalf of children

Section 8 of the Family Law Reform Act 1969 entitles children aged 16 to 18 years to give valid consent to surgical, medical or dental *treatment* without the involvement of parent or guardian. It does not cover the donation of organs, blood or participation in research, nor does it permit a child of this age to *refuse* treatment[19]. Parents or guardians can give valid consent to treatment for children up to the age of majority (18 years). The Children Act 1989 permits either parent to consent if they were married when the child was born, or the mother if they were not; legislation is anticipated which will permit either unmarried parent to consent provided they registered the birth together. Circumstances in which others may consent on behalf of the child are also set out in the Children Act 1989. If the parent or guardian refuses consent and the practitioner considers this is against the best interests of the child, application can be made for the decision to be overruled by the court. Each case is decided on its own merits[20] and the decision is not a foregone conclusion.

Children below the age of 16 years can give valid consent to medical treatment without parental involvement *provided* they have a sufficient maturity and intelligence fully to understand the implications of what is proposed[21], a test widely referred to as 'Gillick competence'. A higher level of maturity and understanding should be sought for more serious procedures. Decisions at this age to refuse recommended treatment should be given due regard but are often overruled[22].

Consent on behalf of the mentally incompetent

Lack of legal competence in the sense defined here can be permanent or transitory. There is currently no legal authority vested in relatives, those holding enduring power of attorney, or even the courts, to consent to treatment on behalf of an incompetent adult[5]. The doctrine of necessity can still be evoked for emergency treatments, and treatment for mental illness (but not coincident physical illness unless a manifestation of the mental illness[23]) can also be given without consent. The Mental Health Act 1983 cannot be invoked to justify treatment or procedures unconnected with the mental condition, even if a patient exhibits apparent irrationality and thoughts contrary to the views of the majority[24]. Only the court can make a declaration as to the lawfulness or otherwise of a proposal to treat a mentally incompetent adult[25]. Treatment without such a declaration is not necessarily 'unlawful', it is merely unprotected by the court. Such a declaration should therefore be sought for contentious proposals such as sterilisation or the withdrawal of supportive treatment[26,27]. The test adopted is that of **best interests**, a concept easy to understand but difficult to define. In the context of an proposal to undertake vasectomy on a man with Down's syndrome, it was held to encompass medical, emotional and all other welfare issues pertaining to the incompetent person[28]. The court declined to comment on whether social considerations or the interests of others should be considered too.

In the absence of a clearly identifiable and accessible source from which to obtain consent on behalf of mentally incompetent adults, patients and practitioners are vulnerable. Courtesy and professional propriety require that practitioners seek information from relatives as to what the incompetent person would have wished, particularly on sensitive questions such as a recommendation not to attempt resuscitation or to withhold or withdraw treatment. Such views are not legally binding but legislation has been proposed to permit the appointment of a proxy (medical attorney) to take treatment decisions on behalf of incompetent adults, including proleptic appointment in case of future incompetence. Specific authorisation would be required for power to seek withdrawal of nutrition and hydration.

Consent for research and teaching

Conflict over research has spawned virtually no English caselaw but current professional recommendations are that particular care should be taken to provide the fullest possible information before subjects are recruited to any research project, therapeutic or non-therapeutic. Information should preferably be in writing and approved before use by the appropriate Research Ethics Committee. The Medical Research Council, Royal College of Physicians and Association of British Pharmaceutical Industries have all offered guidelines and so too have the Medical Defence Organisations. Were a claim to arise from research, it is likely that these professional guidelines would be recognised by the court as defining the appropriate standards of practice. The Law Commission considered it would be unlawful to undertake non-therapeutic research on adults incompetent to consent[29] although professional opinion increasingly accepts such investigation as ethical provided it is 'not against the interests' of the subject. Similarly, professional opinion accepts that participation of children in non-therapeutic research is not necessarily unethical provided

- consent has been obtained from one or both parents *and* a research ethics committee

- the research entails no more than minimal risk

- it does not entail any suffering for the child

- the child does not appear to object.

Gaining and retaining experience is a necessary part of medical education and it is inevitable that trainees, before or after graduation, will be involved in clinical procedures. Consent is not invalidated provided no commitment has been given that a named practitioner will undertake the treatment. It is the *procedure* to which consent has been given. However, the Department of Health recommends that explicit consent should be obtained for the involvement of students[30]. If some element of the procedure is changed or extended beyond usual practice, merely to permit students to learn or experienced practitioners to maintain their expertise, the 'nature' of what has been agreed (ie consented) has been changed. Separate, specific consent should be obtained.

References

1. Appleton & Others v Garrett [1997] 8 Med LR 75.
   Unnecessary dental treatment undertaken for financial gain. Negligence was admitted but claimants also succeeded in an action for 'trespass to the person' (which includes battery) and were awarded aggravated damages.
2. Chatterton v Gerson [1987] 1 All ER 257.
   Neurological damage after a phenol nerve block. Patient deemed to have been informed 'in broad terms' of the nature of the procedure: consent was held to be real and action in battery failed.
3. Re C (Refusal of medical treatment) [1994] 1 All ER 819; noted in [1993] 4 Med LR 238.
   Schizophrenic patient detained at Broadmoor successfully sought an injunction prohibiting amputation of his gangrenous leg without express, written consent. Defines criteria of legal competence to refuse life-saving treatment.
4. Dyer C. BMJ 1998 316:955.
   Parents of 10-year old consented to diagnostic cardiac catheterisation but not balloon dilatation. Practitioner acting in perceived best interest of child attempted balloon dilatation with disastrous consequences. Criticised for exceeding his remit and suspended for 6 months by GMC for professional misconduct.
5. Re T (Adult: refusal of treatment) [1992] 3 Med LR 306.
   Court of Appeal decision confirming the right of competent adults to refuse life-saving treatment and establishing criteria for validity of such a decision. See also *Re MB [1997] 8 Med LR 217* – right to refuse Caesarean section.
6. Poynter v Hillingdon HA BMJ 1997 314:1224.
   Unsuccessful claim for damages on behalf of child severely brain damaged after pioneering cardiac transplant. Parents alleged inadequate information was given and that they were pressurised to consent despite their hostility in principle to transplantation. Information provided was deemed acceptable by the standards of the time.
7. The Centre for Reproductive Medicine v Mrs U [2002] Lloyd's Rep Med 259.
   Widow seeking posthumous insemination contested validity of late husband's withdrawal of consent to use of his sperm after death. Allegation of undue influence sustained but deemed not to have overborne the husband's will.
8. Sidaway v Royal Bethlem and Maudsley Hospital [1985] AC 871.
   Landmark decision by the House of Lords accepting *Bolam principle* – ie professional opinion – as the determinant of how much information is necessary to render consent valid.
9. Rogers v Whittaker [1992] 4 Med LR 79 (decision of High Court of Australia).
   Ophthalmic surgery complicated by sympathetic ophthalmia resulting in virtual blindness. Patient had enquired about possible complications and been reassured. *Bolam principle* rejected: it is for the courts to adjudicate on what is an appropriate standard care. Breach of duty is not to be concluded on expert medical evidence alone.
10. Smith v Tunbridge Wells HA [1994] 5 Med LR 334.
    Impotence after repair of rectal prolapse in a young man. Failure to warn was deemed 'neither reasonable nor responsible', despite some expert opinion to the contrary. See also *Pearce v United Bristol Healthcare NHS Trust [1998] EWCA 865* where Lord Woolf advocates incorporating the 'reasonable patient' test into English law.

11. Reports into paediatric cardiac surgery at Bristol Royal Infirmary and organ retention at Royal Liverpool Childrens' Hospital can be accessed at www.doh.gov.uk/bristolinquiry and www.rlcinquiry.org.uk.

12. BMA Practical Guide to gaining patient consent. British Medical Association, March 2001.
Set of cards summarising essential information relating to specific areas of consent.

13. Good Practice in Consent. HSC 2001/023, Department of Health, November 2001.
Detailed advice from the Department of Health which includes suggested consent forms for specific circumstances. Also available at www.doh.gov.uk See also at this site DoH Consultation Document on the Removal, Retention and Use of Human Organs and Tissues which incorporates recommendations made by the CMO in January 2001.

14. Smith v Barking, Havering & Brentwood HA [1994] 5 Med LR 285.
Unsuccessful action based on alleged failure to give adequate warning. Causation (ie would consent have been withheld if fully informed) to be considered on a subjective basis, but correct to give particular weight to objective assessment unless there are extraneous or additional factors. Can claimant answer reliably after adverse outcome?

15. McAllister v Lewisham & N Southwark HA and Ors [1994] 5 Med LR 343.
Hemiplegia after operative treatment of a cerebral arterio-venous malformation. Had the claimant been warned, she would have declined surgery or postponed it until she had completed a probationary period of employment.

16. Chappel v Hart [1999] Lloyd's Rep Med 223.
Australian case reaching highest appellate court. Successful claim founded on failure adequately to inform of risk of oesophageal perforation during repair of a pharyngeal pouch. Given adequate information the claimant would have had the operation at a later date performed by 'the most experienced surgeon with a record and reputation in the field'. For a similar finding by the Court of Appeal see *Chester v Afshar [2002]* Lloyd's Rep Med 305.

17. Ms B v An NHS Hospital Trust [2002] Lloyd's Rep Med 265.
Vascular abnormality of the high cervical cord resulting in tetraplegia and ventilator dependence. Patient requested that mechanical ventilation be discontinued in accordance with an advance directive framed in general terms. Court not only deemed the patient competent to withhold consent but also awarded nominal damages for trespass to the person. See also revised guidance from the GMC on withholding and withdrawing treatment, July 2002.

18. Ciarlariello *et al* v Schacter *et al* [1991] 2 Med LR 391. (Court of Appeal, Ontario).
During a second cerebral angiogram to locate source of sub-arachnoid haemorrhage, patient insisted test be stopped. It was, and then resumed 10-15 minutes later; quadriplegia followed the final injection. Burden of deciding whether to *commence* the test lay with patient but, once initiated, risk assessment became a matter of medical judgment.

19. Re J (A Minor) (Medical Treatment [1992] 3 Med LR 317.
16-year old with anorexia nervosa. Court has power to overrule refusal by a minor, even if over 16 years. For procedure see *Re O (A Minor) (Medical Treatment) [1993] 4 Med LR 272* (blood transfusion for premature neonate with RDS; parents Jehovah's witnesses); also *R v Portsmouth Hospital NHS Trust [1999] Lloyd's Rep Med 367*: violent conflict between medical staff and family over decision to withhold treatment from disabled 12-year old.

20. Re C (A Minor) (Medical Treatment – Refusal of parental consent) [1997] 8 Med LR 166.
Parents of infant with biliary atresia, both experienced health care workers, refused consent to liver transplant which had been recommended as in child's best interests by three doctors. Strong presumption in favour of preserving life is not an absolute rule and best interests of child not served by forcing major invasive surgery on devoted mother. Compare *Re B (a minor) [1981] 1 WLR 1421*: surgery ordered for duodenal atresia in infant with Down's syndrome.

21. Gillick v W Norfolk and Wisbech AHA [1986] AC 112.
House of Lords ruling on whether, and in what circumstances, children below 16 years can give valid consent to medical treatment, in this case contraception for a 15-year old; mother intractably hostile to lack of parental input.

22. **Re R (A Minor) [1992] 3 Med LR 342.**
    Court of Appeal decision confirming right of parents, guardian or the court to overrule refusal of treatment by a 'Gillick competent' adolescent: a psychotic girl aged 15 years 10 months. See also *BMJ 1999 319:209:* cardiac transplantation sanctioned in a 15-year old who refused consent but whose parents had consented. Judge relied upon view formed by *solicitors* interviewing child that her competence had been eroded by illness.

23. **Fox v Riverside Health Trust [1995] 6 Med LR 181.**
    Feeding is 'treatment' within s145 of Mental Health Act 1983; forced feeding is 'treatment' for anorexia nervosa. See also *R v Collins and Ashworth Hospital Authority ex p Brady [2000] Lloyd's Rep Med 359.*

24. **St George's Healthcare NHS Trust v S [1998] 3 All ER 673.**
    Compulsory admission under Mental Health Act used wrongly to overrule refusal of consent to Caesarean section. Note the unborn child is not 'a person' and does not have rights protected by law.

25. **Re SL (Adult Patient: Sterilisation) [2000] Lloyd's Rep Med 339.**
    Bolam test rejected as the determinant of best interests: it merely provided a range of options. Jurisdiction lies with the court and the doctrine *primum non nocere* should be applied. Simplest measures should be tried first. See also *Re F (Adult Patient: Jurisdiction) [2000] Lloyd's Rep Med 381.*

26. **F v W Berkshire HA [1990] 2 AC 1.**
    'Best interests' determine legality of treatment for adult, incompetent patient – in this case, female sterilisation.

27. **Airedale NHS Trust v Bland [1993] 4 Med LR 39.**
    Legality of withdrawing treatment from a patient in PVS. Reports from both Court of Appeal and House of Lords.

28. **R-B v Official Solicitor [2000] Lloyd's Rep Med 87.**
    Vasectomy for Down's syndrome man not in his best interests, although circumstances could change.

29. **Law Commission Report: Mental Incapacity. 1995 Law Comm 231.**
    One of a series of Law Commission Reports on mental incapacity, including comment on research.

30. **Medical Students in Hospitals. Department of Health HC 91(18).**
    Obtaining explicit consent to participation of medical students in treatment recommended by DoH as 'best practice'.

▶8

Complaints, whistle-blowing and disciplinary proceedings

NHS complaints procedure

Procedures for complaining about services provided by the NHS were rationalised, unified and simplified in 1996 when a revised system[1], based on the recommendations of the Wilson Committee, came into effect. It was intended to be

- ▶ responsive, cost-effective and to enhance quality
- ▶ accessible, impartial and simple
- ▶ swift, confidential and accountable.

Disciplinary proceedings are specifically excluded, although if a complaint raises matters of sufficient significance, relevant information can be passed to managerial and/or professional regulatory bodies for consideration of further action.

The procedure involves two separate stages:

- ▶ Stage I – service providers attempt to resolve each complaint swiftly by
  - ➢ an immediate, often oral, first line response
  - ➢ investigation, followed by a written response from a senior administrative officer.
- ▶ Stage II – complainant has option of asking for a further review which *may* include consideration by a panel with lay chairman and majority of independent members.
- ▶ Referral to the Health Service Commissioner (Ombudsman) is available to complainants dissatisfied with the results of the independent inquiry or the decision not to convene one.

Written reports must be sent to the complainant at each stage unless immediate local resolution, made orally, wholly effective. Reasons must be given if an independent inquiry is refused.

A non-executive director or member of the relevant trust or health authority (the 'convenor') is charged with the responsibility for deciding, in consultation with the proposed lay chairman of the panel, if an independent inquiry is to be set up. Factors to consider are:

- whether any further action short of an inquiry can be taken to satisfy the complainant

- whether all practicable action has been taken already so that an inquiry would add no further value to the process.

Two independent clinical assessors are appointed to the panel if the complaint arises from clinical decisions. Coincident with the introduction of the new complaints procedure, the powers of the Health Ombudsman were extended to include consideration of clinical decision-making.

The complaints system in practice; plans for further reform

Complainants, practitioners and health service managers have all expressed dissatisfaction[2], particularly with the second stage. Resolution takes too long, communication between staff and patients is poor, inquiries are deemed insufficiently independent or perceived to be subject to bias, and there is no mechanism for learning from experience.

The Government has responded by incorporating new recommendations for the handling of complaints in its proposals for greater involvement of the public in the delivery of health care[3]. The Health and Social Care Act 2001 creates a duty on NHS bodies to consult and involve the public, patients and carers in decision-making about the operation of the service. Further legislation is expected to create a National Commission for Patient and Public Involvement in Health (VOICE), with local representation based on each Strategic Health Authority but situated in local authority premises to ensure independence from the health service. All NHS trusts and Primary Care Trusts (PCTs) will have an independent Patients Forum, with power to inspect the work of the trust and representation on its board. All trusts and PCTs must now provide a Patient Advice and Liaison Service (PALS). The staff provide information and assistance to health service users, including an early response to complaints or, if necessary, referral to the Independent Complaints Advocacy Service (ICAS). ICAS will be established and supervised by the National Commission for Patient and Public Involvement in Health and will provide local, direct access for those seeking advice or assistance with the complaints procedure. Provision has also been made for those seeking to complain about treatment in the private sector. The Care Standards Act 2000 creates a National Care Standards Commission. All private medical services must register with the Commission and adhere to its regulatory requirements which include procedures for handling complaints.

These arrangements preserve the separation of procedures for the resolution of complaints and claims. Some commentators would prefer a seamless interface between the two, with power to make *ex gratia* payments up to a defined maximum to some complainants. Separation of procedures for clinical and non-clinical complaints has also been advocated. These conflicts of opinion have yet to be resolved.

Whistle-blowing

In its *Guide to Good Practice*[4] the GMC reminds practitioners of a duty to protect the interests of patients if concerned about the health, conduct or performance of a colleague. It recommends disclosure to appropriate staff from the employing authority such as the medical or nursing director, chief executive or corresponding post-holders. In the absence of local systems or if local action fails to resolve the problem, practitioners are advised to inform the relevant regulatory body. Concerns that those who complied with this professional duty might be victimised were addressed by the Public Interest Disclosure Act 1998 which amends the terms of the Employment Rights Act 1996 to

▶ render invalid contractual terms of employment which seek to prohibit disclosure by employees of information in the public interest, and

▶ to provide remedies for employees treated detrimentally for making such disclosures.

The type of disclosure protected – information 'in the public interest' – is defined in the statute and requires genuine concern about past, current or likely malpractice, including criminal offences and attempts to conceal wrong-doing of any type which should be disclosed. Such disclosures can be made to the employer, a regulatory body or the media without loss of protection. Despite this legislation, many practitioners express disquiet at the possible consequences of discharging the duty to warn of their concerns about the professional competence or behaviour of others[5].

Disciplinary proceedings

The *General Medical Council* is a statutory body which regulates the qualification and registration of medical practitioners under the terms of the Medical Act 1983. Similar provisions exist for dental practitioners, nursing staff and other health care professionals. Responsibility for specialist medical training and standards rests with the Royal Colleges. Specialist accreditation is the responsibility of the Specialist Training Authority (STA) which was created by Statutory Instrument in 1995 to facilitate the free movement of doctors within the European Community.

Five committees of the GMC control fitness to practise, two of which were added to implement the Medical (Professional Performance) Act of 1995. They are

▶ Preliminary Proceedings

▶ Professional Conduct

▶ Health Committee

▶ Assessment Referral

▶ Professional Performance.

Matters which may constitute 'serious professional misconduct' are considered by the Professional Conduct Committee (PCC) after screening by the Preliminary Proceedings Committee. The Professional Conduct Committee has the power to suspend or terminate professional registration. Appeal from a punitive decision by the PCC is to the Privy Council[6]. The Health Committee of the GMC considers fitness to practice if there is evidence of physical or mental ill-health. Its conclusions can be deferred pending the outcome of treatment.

In the wake of several high profile medical scandals, subordinate legislation was introduced in 2000 to widen the powers of the GMC:

▶ An Interim Order Committee can impose interim suspension or specific conditions of practice if public interest or the protection of patients so require.

▶ A minimum of five years must elapse before those struck off the register can reapply.

▶ A statutory duty has been imposed on the GMC to notify employers or bodies with whom a practitioner contracts to provide services when fitness to practice is under consideration.

▶ A power has been created to co-opt non-Council members to GMC committees.

▶ There is now a power to suspend, or place conditions on the registration of practitioners convicted of an offence overseas which would also be a criminal offence in the UK.

The Medical (Professional Performance) Act 1995 came into effect on July 1st 1997 and only performance after that date can be subject to scrutiny. Preliminary assessment covers

▶ attitude

▶ knowledge

▶ clinical and communication skills

▶ clinical records and audit results.

Assessment is carried out by two clinicians from the relevant discipline and a lay member and should be restricted to performance, not overall competence[7]. Depending on the outcome, the practitioner may be required to take action to improve performance, or the case may be referred to the Professional Performance Committee with a view to imposing preconditions or suspending the practitioner's registration. The GMC recommends that referral for assessment should only be used if attempts at local resolution are inappropriate or have failed[8].

Despite attempts to modernise its procedures and image, the GMC is widely perceived as reactionary, and self-serving of the interests of doctors rather than patients. Conversely, a number of disciplinary decisions of the GMC and other regulatory bodies have been subject to successful challenge in the courts[9-11]. The Privy Council has acknowledged that proceedings against the professional status of an appellant attract the protection of Article 6, Human Rights Act 1998[12], and asserted the right to reject recommendations of the Professional Conduct Committee if deemed appropriate.

Further legislative reform of the structure and function of the GMC is imminent, reducing the size of the Council and increasing lay representation from 25 to 40%. Professional revalidation will become a statutory requirement and procedures for assessing fitness to practice are to be simplified. The five committees structure will be abolished and replaced by panels with both medical and lay representation. The panels will consider registration, appeals, fitness to practice and the making of interim orders. They will have the power to terminate professional registration but are also expected to have a broader range of measures at their command than at present. Appeals from a punitive decision by a registration decision panel will be to an appeals panel; appeals to the Privy Council will only be permitted on points of law.

A further level of statutory control on all the health care professions is anticipated. The NHS Reform and Health Care Professions Bill is expected to establish a Council for the Regulation of Health Care Professionals with a supervisory role and, where appropriate, power to appeal decisions taken by the GMC. This would apply particularly in cases of misconduct or fitness to practice where a GMC decision does not appear to offer adequate protection to the public.

Two other recently created statutory bodies will also affect the performance of practitioners. The *National Clinical Assessment Authority* (NCAA) was established in April 2001 and is intended to provide a fast response to concerns about the performance of practitioners to ensure protection for patients and support for doctors. The NCAA can offer recommendations to NHS trusts or employing authorities and, if necessary, report individual cases to the GMC. The Health Act 1999 imposed a duty of clinical governance on trusts which has been extended to Primary Care Trusts by the Health and Social Care Act 2001. As a result, annual appraisal of NHS consultant staff is now mandatory and an employing authority can request external, independent review of an adverse incident or the performance of an individual practitioner. This would normally involve the *Commission for Health Improvement* (CHI) which will then investigate, advise and review the outcome. CHI also has a power to conduct clinical governance inspections of trusts, particularly those suspected of poor performance. Consolidation of the work of the Audit Commission, CHI and the National Care Standards Commission into a single Commission for Healthcare Audit and Inspection (CHAI) is anticipated.

Action by employing authorities

Employing authorities have a right to suspend or dismiss an employee on grounds such as gross misconduct, incompetence, or incapacity (ill-health), and are expected to refer serious matters to the General Medical Council. Recommended procedures are set out in Department of Health Guidelines[13] and, more recently, section 6 of the Health and Social Care Act 2001 creates a power to direct trusts about terms and conditions of employment. Further procedural change is anticipated, including abolition of the right of appeal to the Secretary of State. Suspension on full pay while disciplinary proceedings are in progress is intended as a precaution against possible harm to patients, not as a disciplinary measure. However the perception by most practitioners is of irreversible damage to reputation.

The Department of Health guidelines distinguish 'personal misconduct' which can be handled internally by the trust, and 'professional misconduct' which initially involves assessment by external assessors followed, in serious cases, by an independent inquiry with a legally qualified chairman and both medical and lay representatives. Legal challenge to the choice of procedure has not resulted in consistent recommendations but the Court of Appeal has emphasised that consideration should be given to the terms of the contract of employment and to whether the alleged behaviour could arise from the exercise of medical skills[14].

Disciplinary proceedings against general practitioners have been revised by recent legislation which permits a Health Authority to suspend or remove practitioners from local lists on the basis of inefficiency, fraud or unsuitability. Health Authorities must maintain lists of GPs, including locums and deputies, and only those registered on the list can be employed. GPs must also declare to their employing authority any criminal conviction or investigation by another authority. NHS Tribunals have been abolished and replaced by a new statutory body, the Family Health Services Appeal Authority (FHSAA). This hears appeals against decisions on removal, has the power to disqualify a GP on a national basis, and can also do so on application by a health authority. It remains to be seen how far this plethora of new legislative bodies and procedures will redress the current public perception of medicine as an ill-regulated profession[15].

References

1. Acting on Complaints. DOH 1995.
   Government's proposals for revision to complaints handling, circulated to health authorities as EL (95) 37, responding to *Being Heard, DOH 1994*: report of Wilson Committee on NHS complaints procedures.
2. Reforming the NHS complaints procedure: a listening document. DoH, September 2001.
   Available at www.doh.gov.uk/nhscomplaintsreform/listening.htm
3. Shifting the balance of power within the NHS: securing delivery. DoH, July 2001.
   Available at www.doh.gov.uk/shiftingthebalance
4. Guide to Good Practice, paragraphs 26–28. General Medical Council 2001.
   Duty to protect patients – what practitioners should do if concerned about a colleague.
5. Yamey G. Protecting whistleblowers. BMJ 2000 320:70.
   Report of a BMA conference on how to protect and empower whistleblowers.
6. Roylance v General Medical Council (on appeal to the Privy Council from the Professional Conduct Committee) [1999] Lloyd's Rep Med 139.
   Unsuccessful appeal by medically qualified Chief Executive of Bristol Royal Infirmary against

finding of serious professional misconduct while engaged in administrative duties, and subsequent erasure from the medical register.

7. Krippendorf v General Medical Council [2001] Lloyd's Rep Med 9.
   Professional performance is to be assessed on work actually done, not competence to perform work never undertaken. The assessment panel had erred in not exploring the substance of the specific complaints.

8. Maintaining Good Medical Practice. General Medical Council, July 1998.
   See also specific guidance from GMC in Performance Procedures: a guide to the new arrangements July 1998, and Management in Health Care: the role of doctors. General Medical Council, December 1999.

9. R v GMC *ex parte* Toth [2000] Lloyd's Rep Med 368 and R v GMC *ex parte* Richards [2001] Lloyd's Rep Med 47.
   Judicial analysis of the role of the preliminary screener (*Toth*) and preliminary proceedings committee (*Richards*). Function of both is restricted and had been exceeded in both cases. More judicial criticism of GMC procedures was raised in *Holmes, Dean & Dean v GMC & Drs Rahman and Sengupta [2001] Lloyd's Rep Med 366*.

10. Stefan v General Medical Council [1999] Lloyd's Rep Med 90.
    Application to be given reasons for continued suspension. There is a common law, but not statutory, duty to give sufficient information to advise practitioner in broad terms the reasons for the decision. Similar conclusion reached in *Selvanathan v GMC [2001] Lloyd's Rep Med 1*, although reasons are not needed for findings of fact.

11. Dad v General Dental Council [2000] Lloyd's Rep Med 299.
    Conviction for a motoring offence did not render practitioner unfit to practise as a dentist. Professional disciplinary proceedings should not impose a second penalty.

12. Ghosh v General Medical Council [2001] Lloyd's Rep Med 433.
    Professional misconduct proceedings involve a determination of civil rights and obligations and consequently attract protection of Article 6 of European Convention on Human Rights as scheduled in Human Rights Act 1998. Privy Council would respect GMC Committee's finding but would not defer to it more than was warranted. PC entitled to consider whether GMC sanction was disproportionate and, if so, substitute another or remit for reconsideration. See also *Carroll v Council for Professions Supplementary To Medicine (Radiographers' Board) [2002] Lloyd's Rep Med 71*. Although this was an unsuccessful appeal against erasure from the register, the report *opens* with a useful commentary on the implications of the Human Rights Act 1998, the greater willingness of the Privy Council to intervene, the need for penalties to be proportionate to the offence and to be supported by reasons.

13. Health Circular (90) 9. Department of Health, 1990.
    Recommendations for conduct of disciplinary hearings into conduct or competence of hospital practitioners. Annexe (C) sets out the procedure for appeal against dismissal.

14. Saeed v Royal Wolverhampton Hospitals NHS Trust [2001] Lloyd's Rep Med 111.
    Authoritative (Court of Appeal) ruling on tests to be applied to determine if alleged misconduct is personal or professional and hence procedure to be adopted under HC (90)9. See also *Skidmore v Dartford & Gravesham NHS Trust [2002] Lloyd's Rep Med 299*.

15. Irvine D. The performance of doctors: the new professionalism. Lancet 1999 353:1174.
    GMC President reminds practitioners: professional independence is a privilege requiring competent self-regulation. See also *Walshe K. The rise of regulation in the NHS. BMJ 2002 324:967*.

▶9
Doctors and the coroner's court

Proceedings in the coroner's court are governed by statute (The Coroners Act 1988), supplemented by The Coroners Rules 1984. Coroners are appointed by a county council, metropolitan or borough council and are identified by the district for which they are responsible. The majority are solicitors but some are medically or dually qualified; a minimum of five years' experience is required in either case. Only a minority are full-time coroners.

Apart from an historical role to investigate the finding of treasure trove, the duty of the coroner is restricted to the investigation of certain deaths. He is charged with a duty to make enquiry

▶ when informed that the body of a person is lying within his jurisdiction *and*

▶ there is reasonable cause to suspect that the death was

▶ either violent or unnatural

▶ or sudden and of unknown cause

▶ or occurred in prison

▶ or in such place or circumstances as to require an inquest pursuant to any other Act.

It is not necessary for the death itself to have occurred within the jurisdiction.

A jury *can* be called for any inquest but *must* be called if the death occurred

▶ in prison

▶ while the deceased was in police custody or resulted from injury caused by a police officer in the execution of his duty

▶ as a consequence of accident, poisoning or disease, notice of which is required to be given under any Act eg Health and Safety at Work Act 1974

▶ in circumstances the continuance or possible recurrence of which is prejudicial to the health or safety of the public or any section thereof.

The jury at an inquest is composed of not less than seven and not more than eleven jurors.

Duty to inform the coroner

Medical practitioners commonly sign a 'death certificate' but this does no more than certify the cause of death. Note that when criteria for brain stem death have been fulfilled, the time of death is deemed to be no later than when the first set of tests was completed[1]. The legal death certificate is issued by the Registrar of Births and Deaths. There is no *obligation* on the medical practitioner to report deaths which could lie within the criteria enumerated above, but it is courteous and sensitive to do so. The Registrar will report the death to the coroner if he is not prepared to issue a formal death certificate on the information received.

Death should be reported to the coroner in the following circumstances:

▶ the cause is unknown

▶ the practitioner has not attended the deceased during his last illness

▶ the practitioner *neither* attended the deceased during the last 14 days before death *nor* saw the body after death

▶ death occurred during an operation or before recovery from the effects of an anaesthetic

▶ death was caused by industrial disease or poisoning

▶ any death believed to unnatural or caused by violence, neglect or abortion.

Some of these terms are imprecise, particularly 'unnatural' when applied to the elderly and infirm. However, a coroner informed of such a death has a *discretion* to dispense with an inquest, with or without a post mortem examination, and can then notify the Registrar of his decision. Informal consultation with the coroner will clarify whether or not a death should be reported.

The coroner's post mortem examination

The coroner has jurisdiction over the body once a death has been reported to him. He can order a post mortem examination to be undertaken by a practitioner of his choice. When death occurs in the course of medical treatment, particularly if anxieties have been expressed about the standard of care, the post mortem is usually carried out at another location by an independent pathologist. The pathologist's report is addressed to the coroner and is confidential unless he authorises disclosure. Post mortem material *of potential relevance to the cause of death* can be retained at the discretion of the pathologist but only for such period as the coroner thinks fit.

The inquest

An inquest is an inquiry, not a trial. However, grievances as well as grief are often manifest and, particularly if there are legal representatives, the questioning can be quite hostile. It is up to the coroner to restrict questions to the matters to be explored, namely

▶ who the deceased was

▶ when, where and how the deceased came by his death.

The question 'how' is interpreted restrictively to mean 'by what means' rather than 'in what broad circumstances'[2] but the coroner is still expected to make full, fair and fearless enquiry[3]. Resolution of these apparently conflicting requirements is a matter for the coroner's discretion.

Most inquests are opened and adjourned soon after the death and only evidence of identity is submitted. This suffices for the coroner to provide relatives with a certificate for burial, cremation or removal of the body outside England. Disposal is not authorised if criminal charges are likely.

The inquest is resumed after relevant witness statements have been obtained. The proceedings are formal but less so than in other courts. The coroner examines on oath or affirmation those witnesses who, in his opinion, can contribute evidence relevant to the questions listed above. The witnesses can then be cross-examined by 'properly interested persons' or their representatives, for example the family of the deceased, or the police if the death occurred in custody. Medical practitioners may be called upon to give evidence concerning

▶ the post mortem examination

▶ the deceased's health and habits during life (eg smoking, drug or alcohol addiction)

▶ medical aspects of the deceased's terminal illness.

No witness is obliged to answer any question tending to incriminate him, and the coroner is prohibited from framing a verdict in such a way as to appear to determine any question of civil liability, or of criminal liability on the part of a named person. If, during the course of an inquest, it appears to the coroner that a person may be charged with a specific offence such as murder or manslaughter, he must adjourn the hearing and report to the Director of Public Prosecutions. This procedure is followed if the coroner considers there could be a finding of criminal negligence.

Inquests into deaths occurring in the course of, or as a result of, medical treatment are the source of most concern to practitioners. They or their hospital are likely to be represented by a medical defence organisation or hospital solicitor, particularly if grievances are suspected or the family is to be legally represented (despite the non-availability of legal aid for representation at inquests). Disclosure of hospital notes, records and internal inquiry reports is covered in chapter 6. A witness who fails to attend when summoned may be found guilty of contempt of court[4] and reluctant witnesses may be served with a subpoena. It is also an offence to refuse to answer questions, withhold information, or give evidence known to be erroneous while on oath.

The coroner's verdict

The verdict is the totality of the findings made by the coroner or the jury but the term is often used merely to refer to the conclusion. Certain terms are recommended, the most common being

▶ death from natural causes

▶ industrial disease

▶ dependent or non-dependent abuse of drugs

▶ accident or misadventure

▶ suicide

▶ unlawful killing

▶ open verdict.

Note that a finding of still-birth negates the rest of the inquiry – the infant has not had life independent from its mother. Suicide and unlawful killing both require proof beyond reasonable doubt whereas all other verdicts can be made on the balance of probabilities. An open verdict is reserved for cases where there is insufficient evidence to reach any of the other conclusions.

Accident or misadventure in the context of deaths related to medical treatment

There is judicial authority for the view that the term 'misadventure' is obsolete[5] but many coroners continue to use it. Defined as the unintended adverse outcome of an intentional, lawful act, it is well suited to many deaths occurring in the course of treatment. It does *not* carry any implication of negligence, nor does it refute the possibility of such a finding in a civil court[6]. Many families find the term more acceptable than mere 'accident', with its connotation that the cause of death was independent of any human intervention when it manifestly was not.

A descriptive verdict

When death occurs in the course of a potentially fatal condition and medical intervention fails to prevent the death, a conclusion of 'natural causes' is correct. If the circumstances surrounding the death are exceptional, the verdict can incorporate a brief, neutral factual statement[7].

'Lack of care' as a rider to the verdict

This is a phrase where the strict legal definition of 'care' is of paramount importance. It refers to care in the narrow, physical sense and has ***nothing to do with negligence or breach of duty***[3].

The concept is of 'neglect' – gross failure to provide food, liquid, shelter, warmth or basic medical attention for someone in a dependent position who cannot provide it for himself. Neglect (or self-neglect) should not form part of the verdict unless a clear and direct causal connection with the death can be established. Despite these defining criteria, attempts are still made by legal representatives appearing for families of patients dying in contentious circumstances to persuade the coroner to find 'lack of care'. Such applications rarely succeed but may herald a civil claim, or reflect a wish for public obloquy when civil action is impractical, usually for financial reasons. A finding of lack of care requires evidence of *absence* of care, not possibly erroneous care[8,9]. The form available to the coroner for recording the findings of the inquest ('the inquisition') suggests that the phrase 'and the cause of death was aggravated by lack of care/self-neglect' can *only* be added when the finding is of death from natural causes, industrial disease, dependence on drugs or non-dependent abuse of drugs.

This interpretation has been challenged[10] and, in appeals arising from inquests into two deaths in custody[11], it was held that a verdict of neglect is permissible if the coroner considers such a finding could serve to reduce the risk of repetition of the circumstances giving rise to the death in question.

Recommendations by the coroner

The coroner, but not a coroner's jury, has power to refer matters to the appropriate authority if by so doing it would enable changes to be made to prevent repetition of similar fatalities.

Challenge to decisions of the coroner

Application to challenge the decision of a coroner, including a decision not to hold an inquest[12,13], is made either by seeking leave for judicial review or by the statutory power of obtaining the *fiat* of the Attorney-General. The appeal is heard by the Divisional Court, a sub-division of the High Court usually constituted by a Lord Justice of Appeal and a High Court Judge. There is potential for appeal from the Divisional Court to the Court of Appeal. In general the courts are reluctant to order a new inquest unless it is likely that a different conclusion would be reached[14].

Home Office Review

Major changes in the content and conduct of inquests are anticipated after completion of a fundamental review initiated by the Home Office. It seeks to address concerns raised by the inquiries into paediatric cardiac surgery at Bristol Royal Infirmary, the retention of organs at the Royal Liverpool Children's Hospital, and the murders committed by Dr Harold Shipman.

References

1. Re A [1992] 3 Med LR 303.
   Brain stem death after alleged non-accidental injury in child of 19 months. Court has jurisdiction to declare patient dead for all legal as well as medical purposes, from date of completion of first set of tests for brain stem death.
2. R v HM Coroner for Western District of East Sussex *ex parte* Homberg, Roberts and Manners (1994) 158 JP 357.
   Challenge to conduct of an inquest into deaths caused by arson. The inquiry must focus on matters directly causative of death. 'How' means by what means, not in what broad circumstances.

3. **R v HM Coroner for N Humberside** *ex parte* Jamieson [1994] 3 WLR 82.
Court of Appeal hearing arising from suicide of a prisoner. Extensive review of history and function of coroner's court is followed by a summary of current role and, most importantly, definitive criteria for a finding of 'lack of care'.

4. **Re Dr AS Ryan** (1984) 148 JP 569.
Police surgeon summoned to give evidence at an inquest failed to arrive in time and was ordered to pay a fine. Decision challenged successfully – he had not been properly summoned and could give good explanation for delay.

5. **R v HM Coroner for Portsmouth** *ex parte* Anderson [1987] 1 WLR 1640.
Death of a serviceman from hyperpyrexia; finding of 'accidental death' challenged unsuccessfully. The distinction between 'accident' and 'misadventure' was deemed to be without purpose or effect. Note however the acceptance in *R v Southwark Coroner ex parte Fields 1998 162 JP 411* of misadventure as a sub-heading of accidental death.

6. **R v HM Coroner for Birmingham & Solihull** *ex parte* Cotton (1996) 160 JP 123.
Challenge to verdict of natural causes: hospital death from pneumonia in sedated patient with alcoholic liver disease, gastro-intestinal bleeding and smoking-related lung damage. Purpose of an inquest is to discover the cause of death, not get a negligence claim on its feet. Questions of medical negligence should be tried by a Judge on a pleaded case.

7. **R v HM Coroner for Birmingham & Solihull** *ex parte* Benton [1997] 8 Med LR 362.
2-year old with laryngo-tracheo-bronchitis died from bilateral tension pneumothoraces and surgical emphysema soon after emergency bronchoscopy undertaken after prolonged delay in securing hospital admission. Jury permitted only to consider verdict of death from natural causes which they endorsed by majority of 8:1. Challenge to verdict upheld only in so far as possibility of accident/misadventure should have been left for jury to consider. Finding of 'natural causes' was quashed and a descriptive account was to be given for cause of death. New inquest not ordered.

8. **R v HM Coroner for Surrey** *ex parte* Wright [1997] 1 All ER 823.
Fit Afro-Carribean 27-year old died from cerebral damage after anoxic incident during GA for dental extraction. Verdict of accidental death challenged on several grounds including "If this is not a case of lack of care, what is?" Verdict upheld; no new inquest ordered. Re-emphasis on 'matters of negligence are better decided in a civil action'.

9. **R v HM Coroner for Wiltshire** *ex parte* Clegg (1997) 161 JP 521.
Deceased took an overdose of aspirin and died about 12 hours after admission to hospital. Coroner did not receive, or call for, any medical evidence relating to hospital admission, a fact known to hospital staff. Verdict of suicide. Two years later, independent review set up in response to parental complaints, was highly critical of all aspects of management. New inquest then sought. Court expressed concern at lack of obligation to volunteer information, considered finding of neglect contributing to the death *might* have been made, but this did not warrant new inquest.

10. **R v HM Coroner for Coventry** *ex parte* O'Reilly (1996) 160 JP 749.
Deceased had fallen at home and, believed to be drunk, was taken into custody. Transferred to hospital 13 hours later, deeply unconscious, where CT showed large intra-cerebral haematoma. Challenge to verdict of accidental death upheld and new inquest ordered. No reason in principle or logic why accidental death aggravated by lack of care should not be appropriate if circumstances justify, despite obstacle of proving a causal link.

11. **R (Amin) v Secretary of State for Home Department; R (Middleton) v Coroner for West Somersetshire** [2002] Lloyd's Rep Med 187.
Two appeals, heard together, arising from inquests into deaths in custody (one murder by fellow inmate, one suicide). Court of Appeal held that a verdict of neglect *was* permissible when the inquest was, in practice, the means of discharging the state's duty under Article 2 of the Human Rights Act 1998 (to protect the right to life), and the coroner considered a finding of neglect might reduce the risk of repetition – in other words, eliminate a system error.

12. **R v HM Coroner for Avon** *ex parte* Smith (1998) 162 JP 403.
Coroner declined to hold an inquest into death of 14-year old in hospital, admitted with cerebral symptoms. CT, which showed cerebellar haemorrhage, not performed for 10 hours despite concern of parents who had earlier lost a son from a 'cerebral episode'. Internal and external enquiries exonerated hospital staff; coroner stated no grounds for inquest because death was 'not unnatural'. Inquest ordered – question of 'natural causes' warranted investigation.

13. **R v HM Coroner for Inner London North** *ex parte* **Touche [2001] Lloyd's Rep Med 327.**

    Maternal death from cerebral haemorrhage occurring after Caesarean section for twins. Initially certified as death from natural causes, it subsequently transpired there had been prolonged delay in recognising severe post-operative maternal hypertension. Application to compel the coroner to hold an inquest succeeded at first instance and on appeal: there was evidence to suggest neglect may have contributed to the death, so rendering it 'unnatural'. A combination of unexpectedness and culpable human failing, albeit not sufficient to amount to neglect, will make a death unnatural.

14. **R v HM Coroner for Derbyshire (Scarsdale)** *ex parte* **Fletcher (1992) 156 JP 522.**

    Deceased had worked as a miner from age 14–50 years. Died aged 65 from chronic obstructive pulmonary disease and congestive cardiomyopathy. Reported to pneumoconiosis medical panel who concluded pneumoconiosis neither caused nor materially accelerated death. Verdict of natural causes. During investigation to secure compensation, new expert report suggested pneumoconiosis *was* a contributory factor. Unusually, a new inquest was ordered. Normally mere differences of opinion between experts do not suffice: new *evidence* not new *interpretation* is needed.

►10
Doctors and the criminal law

The essential difference between a civil and a criminal offence is that one reflects conflict between two or more individuals and is aimed at securing recompense, whereas the other is conflict between an individual and society with a view to punishment. Minor criminal offences are dealt with in the **Magistrates Court** but matters of greater importance are heard in the **Crown Court** by a judge sitting with a jury whose members are the representatives of society. Doctors are not immune from criminality but prosecutions brought against individual practitioners are considered here only in the context of criminal charges arising from deaths associated with clinical practice.

Conviction for a criminal offence requires proof beyond reasonable doubt that

► the person charged has carried out an unlawful act (*'actus reus'*) and

► in doing so had the necessary guilty state of mind (*'mens rea'*).

Specific 'elements' for each offence define the unlawful act and the necessary guilty state of mind. Both must be made out if the prosecution is to succeed (cf the civil claimant's need to establish both breach of duty and causation), but liability can still be diminished or even avoided if the defendant can advance a valid defence (for example, provocation in the context of murder).

The standard of proof required in a criminal case – beyond reasonable doubt – is higher than the balance of probabilities which suffices for civil actions. Another practical distinction is that the legal rules of evidence are observed more stringently in criminal matters. The phrase 'beyond reasonable doubt' does not mean 'beyond a shadow of doubt'. A remote possibility, which is not in the least probable, does not create 'reasonable doubt'. The judge directs the jury on the standard required, often telling them 'they must be satisfied so that they are sure'.

Homicide

Homicide is the unlawful killing of a human being, identified in the context of infants as a life independent from the mother. Murder and manslaughter are both homicide, distinguished by the state of mind of the defendant and the perceived culpability so determined.

The cause of death must be attributable to the unlawful act, as a matter of fact and of law. Causation in fact is determined by the 'but for' test – but for the act in question, would the victim have died? Causation in law requires exploration of the closeness of the link between the act and the death. Was the act a substantial and operating factor? An example helps to explain this concept – a victim is knocked unconscious and left on the shore where he drowns when the tide comes in. The factual cause of death is drowning: the cause in law is the act of the defendant. Undue vulnerability of the victim (the 'eggshell skull' rule) does not exonerate the perpetrator.

The importance of the distinction between causation in fact and in law is apparent when considering the role of medical interventions. Thus two assailants, each convicted of murder, appealed on the grounds that a subsequent medical decision to withdraw mechanical ventilation caused the deaths[1]. Both appeals failed. Even clinical negligence as an intervening event will not *necessarily* displace responsibility for an unlawful death (eg murder)[2]. Similarly, when considering an application for a declaration that withdrawal of mechanical ventilation from a patient with exceptionally severe Guillain-Barre syndrome would not be unlawful[3], a New Zealand court accepted that the cause of death would be the disease and not the act of withdrawal, *provided* the decision to withdraw ventilation had been made in accordance with good medical practice. Thus the *propriety* of the medical act which intervenes between initiating event or illness and the fatal outcome is to be taken into consideration when considering the legal cause of death, as well as the *magnitude* of the contribution of each element to the death.

Intention to kill or *to cause serious injury* is a prerequisite for a conviction of murder. Primary or specific purpose intent exists when a person sets out to secure an objective by whatever means lie within his power. Secondary intent (also known as indirect or foresight intent) is a presumption: a man is presumed to intend the consequences of his act if the outcome is a virtual certainty and he is aware, when acting, that this is so. Evidence must be adduced in each case to satisfy the jury to the requisite standard that these conditions were, in fact, fulfilled. An important distinction must be drawn between intention and motive. Intention refers to what the actor seeks to achieve; motive is the reason for acting. A benevolent motive does not displace a criminal conviction for murder if the intention to kill is made out at trial[4].

Voluntary manslaughter is the likely verdict if a defendant is found guilty of causing death and of having the intention to kill but has successfully pleaded one of a number of defences, usually provocation or diminished responsibility. The significance lies in the sentence. Murder carries a mandatory life sentence whereas sentencing for manslaughter is at the discretion of the judge.

Involuntary manslaughter is a verdict which follows a finding that the defendant caused the death, but without any intention to kill or cause serious injury. It includes death occurring as the result of an unlawful act or, most commonly in the context of medical manslaughter, as a consequence of what has variously been described as 'recklessness' or 'gross negligence'. The discussion here is restricted to gross negligence in the discharge of professional responsibilities.

Manslaughter by gross negligence

It is arguable that deaths arising as a result of medical treatment can be distinguished from the usual case of homicide because it is the defendant's professional obligations which require him to deal with a pre-existing danger which is not of his own making. This philosophy lay behind the original definition of gross (ie criminal) negligence[5] which required

- ▶ the existence of a duty of care

- ▶ breach of the duty

- ▶ death occurring as a consequence of the breach of duty

- ▶ negligence which went beyond a mere matter of compensation between the parties.

The first three elements of this test are identical to those set out in chapter 2 as the basis for a *civil* claim in negligence. The fourth is the dimension which adds criminality – showing such a high degree of disregard for the safety of others that it amounts to a crime against the State and is deserving of punishment.

After some years when 'gross negligence' was regarded by the courts as synonymous with recklessness, the importance of specific criteria for a finding of gross negligence in the discharge of professional responsibilities was re-emphasised by the Court of Appeal in the course of three appeals, heard simultaneously, against convictions for manslaughter by an electrician, two junior doctors, and a locum anaesthetist[6]. Two of the appeals succeeded but the third did not. The third appellant appealed, unsuccessfully, to the House of Lords[7] when the criteria for a finding of involuntary manslaughter by breach of duty suggested by the Court of Appeal were confirmed as

- the existence of a duty

- breach of the duty causing death

- gross negligence which a jury considers justifies a criminal conviction.

The third of these is the only one which differs in terminology, if not in meaning, from the original definition of 'gross negligence'. A jury is entitled to make a finding of gross negligence if evidence is adduced to show that the defendant

- was indifferent to an obvious risk of injury to health *or*

- had actual foresight of the risk but determined nevertheless to run it *or*

- appreciated the risk and intended to avoid it but displayed such a high degree of negligence in the attempted avoidance as the jury considered justified conviction *or*

- displayed inattention or failure to advert to a serious risk which went beyond 'mere inadvertence' in respect of an obvious and important matter which the defendant's duty demanded he should address.

Given these directions, it is the *jury* which decides whether the evidence suffices to fulfil one or more of the criteria and, if so, whether the charge of gross negligence has been made out. Charges of manslaughter by medical negligence have increased in number in recent years[8] but the conviction rate is low by comparison with manslaughter cases generally, possibly because of the difficulty of proving, beyond reasonable doubt, that medical error caused the death[9]. It remains to be seen whether the imposition of a duty of clinical governance on trusts will lead to charges of corporate killing under the terms of proposed legislation.

Criminal liability for end-of-life decisions

The conviction of a caring doctor for attempted murder[4], followed shortly by a House of Lords decision that it would not be unlawful to withdraw artificial nutrition and hydration from a patient in persistent vegetative state[10], led to the setting up of a House of Lords Committee[11] to consider the ethical, legal and clinical implications of end-of-life decision-making. The recommendations of the Committee were conservative:

▶ the law should not be changed to permit active euthanasia

▶ the right of competent patients to refuse medical treatment was strongly endorsed

▶ the law on suicide[12] should not be changed

▶ there should be no new offence of 'mercy-killing'

▶ the mandatory life-sentence for murder should be dropped.

All but the last of the recommendations were accepted by government. The Committee also acknowledged that it is lawful – indeed proper – to administer drugs to relieve pain notwithstanding an awareness of the probability that they will hasten death, a view confirmed in caselaw both before and after the report was published[13,14]. The essential legal element is the intention of the practitioner – if the primary intention is to relieve suffering, the *mens rea* for a finding of murder is absent. The practitioner may foresee that death is virtually certain after, and perhaps as a consequence of the treatment, but the presumption that he therefore intends the death is refuted by evidence that his primary intent is to benefit the patient. Some regard this argument as specious – and perhaps in practice it is.

Two high-profile cases, both considered since the Human Rights Act came into force, have endorsed the stance taken in 1994. Euthanasia or assisted suicide remain unlawful[15] but action leading even to inevitable death is not necessarily unlawful if justified by the magnitude of benefit secured thereby – in this case survival of one of conjoined twins[16]. The doctrine of necessity was invoked to justify the lesser of two evils (death of one rather than both twins).

Termination of life-support is followed by death in stark, temporal proximity. The practitioner is protected from a charge of murder if the decision accords with good medical practice. There is no obligation to continue treatment deemed to be futile or not in the patient's best interests, but evidence must be available to support this contention[17]. Particular difficulty is associated with the chronic stable condition of persistent vegetative state. The House of Lords has accepted that 'treatment' can include nutrition and hydration when provided by artificial means[10]. In that case, the severity of the neurological damage was deemed such that either the patient had no best interests or they were not served by continued treatment. However, the decision was not to be used as a precedent –

parliament, not the courts, should be responsible for formulating principle. Thus a declaration by the court should be obtained if the withdrawal of nutrition and hydration is contemplated from a profoundly damaged but physiologically stable patient[18]. Perceived conflict over the status of nutrition and hydration as 'treatment' or 'basic humanitarian care' means that particular care is necessary before taking such a step in any circumstances[19]. The present position is unsatisfactory because the limits of legality are not clearly defined. A private member's bill – Medical Treatment (Prevention of Euthanasia) – which sought to prohibit the withholding or withdrawing of medical treatment, including hydration and nutrition, when this would bring about the death of the patient, was rejected but legislation is anticipated to permit extension of enduring power of attorney to include clinical decision-making. Withholding or withdrawing medical treatment has also been considered by the English courts within the framework of the Human Rights Act 1998 but no change of principle has emerged[20,21].

Withholding treatment is acceptable practice *provided* the treating practitioner genuinely and for good reason believes it to be in the best interests of the patient to do so[22]. The court will not dictate what is appropriate treatment[23]. The apparent discrepancy between the court's power to overrule parental decisions to withhold consent and its reluctance to order treatment requested by parents but resisted by the practitioner, reflects the principle that what is done should be in the best interests of the patient and that is primarily a matter of expert opinion. Practical guidance on withholding and withdrawing treatment was published by the General Medical Council in August 2002[24].

The law as a vehicle for social change

In 1939 an eminent gynaecologist announced that he intended to terminate the pregnancy of a 14-year old victim of gang rape. He duly did so at a prestigious London hospital. He was prosecuted and acquitted on a technicality of interpretation of the then-relevant statute[25]. The case focussed attention on the fact that abortion, although unlawful, was widely practised, albeit in circumstances which were often unhygienic and dangerous. Subsequent caselaw reflected this liberal statutory interpretation and was followed ultimately in 1967 by the first Abortion Act. A number of controversial social and ethical issues have since prompted responsive legislation, often without a legal test case. Some examples include The Human Organ Transplantation Act 1989, The Human Fertilisation and Embryology Act

1990 and the Surrogacy Arrangements Act 1985. The law – whether it is defined in the courts or established by legislation – sets the limits of what is deemed to be acceptable practice. It is not immutable but can and does change in response to new developments or social pressures. There is no reason why medical practitioners, parliamentarians or judges should be the sole arbiters of ethical dilemmas, but rules need to be set and the law is empowered to fulfil that role. It is the duty of all citizens – including medical practitioners – to abide by the law and, if the law assists in defining the boundaries of acceptable medical practice, its intervention is to be welcomed, not feared.

References

1. R v Malcherek; R v Steel [1981] 2 All ER 422.
   Discontinuing mechanical ventilation did not suffice to interrupt the chain of causation between initial assault upon each of two victims and their subsequent death. Appeals against convictions for murder failed.
2. R v Cheshire [1991] 1 WLR 844.
   Failure to recognise tracheal stricture the proximate cause of death of a victim who had been shot 5 weeks earlier. Defendant's appeal against conviction of murder was unsuccessful.
3. Auckland Area Health Board v Attorney-General [1993] 4 Med LR 239.
   New Zealand declaration that it would be lawful to withdraw mechanical ventilation from a patient severely affected by Guillain Barre syndrome. Questions explored were whether death was caused by the disease (yes) or the withdrawal of ventilation, and whether mechanical ventilation was a necessity of life (not in these circumstances).
4. R v Cox (1992) 12 BMLR 38; (and see legal commentary BMJ 1992 305:731).
   Conviction for attempted murder (cause of death unproven because body had been cremated before charges were brought). Consultant Rheumatologist administered intravenous potassium chloride to a woman terminally ill from chronic rheumatoid arthritis, in 'uncontrollable' pain, who begged to die and whose family supported her decision.
5. R v Bateman (1925) LJKB 791.
   Gross, fatal, pelvic visceral injury during attempted home delivery. Criteria for gross negligence defined.
6. R v Holloway; R v Adomako; R v Prentice & Sullman [1993] 4 Med LR 304.
   This report does not include the facts of R v Holloway – an electrician whose faulty wiring of a central heating system caused death by electrocution – but the Court of Appeal set out principles applying to all three cases. The anaesthetic death involved failure to recognise disconnection of the ventilator; the third case arose from a fatal injection of vincristine into the theca in a patient receiving regular intrathecal methotrexate and intravenous vincristine. The appeals of Holloway, Prentice and Sullman were allowed, their convictions being quashed. Adomako's appeal failed.
7. R v Adomako [1994] 5 Med LR 277.
   Appeal to the House of Lords by the unsuccessful appellant (an anaesthetist) from (6) above also failed. It is sufficient to direct the jury to adopt the criteria for gross negligence set out by the Court of Appeal in this case.
8. Ferner R; Medication errors that have led to manslaughter charges. BMJ 2000; 321:1212–16.
   Review confined to medication errors. Incidence of charges of medical manslaughter have increased from about one case every four years (1972–90) to almost two each year (1990–2000). This reflects a policy decision by the Crown Prosecution Service to prosecute cases of suspected gross negligence or recklessness in the workplace. See also BMJ 2002; 325:63 for summary of more recent cases.

9. Dyer C. Surgeons cleared of manslaughter after removing wrong kidney. BMJ 2002 325:6.

    Delayed death from multiple organ failure after removal of sole functioning kidney in an elderly man. Trial for manslaughter collapsed because pathologist 'could not be sure' the nephrectomy had caused the death.

10. Airedale NHS Trust v Bland [1993] 4 Med LR 39.

    House of Lords decision that withdrawal of artificial nutrition and hydration from a patient in persistent vegetative state would not be unlawful. Their Lordships specifically stated the decision should *not* be regarded as a precedent.

11. Select Committee on Medical Ethics, House of Lords Report. HMSO 1994.

    Legal and ethical analysis of end of life decisions. Law should not be changed to permit active euthanasia. Offence of 'mercy-killing' not recommended; suggestion to drop mandatory life sentence for murder rejected by government.

12. Suicide Act 1961

    Suicide is no longer a criminal offence but section 2 preserves aiding and abetting suicide as an offence.

13. R v Bodkin Adams [1957] Crim LR 365.

    GP acquitted of murder by administration of increasing doses of opiates to elderly patients with a view to personal gain. See also *R v Arthur (1981) 12 BMLR 1*; acquittal of consultant paediatrician charged with attempted murder by prescribing 'dihydrocodeine and nursing care only' for a neonate with Down's syndrome, rejected by her mother.

14. Dyer C. Brit Med J 1999 318:1306.

    Unwise public declaration by a GP that he had helped a number of patients to have pain-free deaths led to prosecution for murder. Unanimous verdict of 'not guilty'. GP's considerate treatment was applauded by the judge. See *Gillon R, Doyal L Brit Med J 1999 318:1431* for discussion of ethical doctrine of 'double effect'.

15. R v Director of Public Prosecutions *ex parte* Pretty and Secretary of State for the Home Department [2001] 63 BMLR 1.

    Patient with terminal motor neurone disease sought a declaration that no criminal charge would be brought against her husband if he assisted her to die when she considered life intolerable. Framed in terms of the Human Rights Act 1998, the application failed at first instance and on appeal to the Divisional Court, House of Lords and European Court (European Court Reference 2346/02; 29.04.02).

16. Re A (Minors) (Conjoined Twins: Separation) [2000] Lloyd's Rep Med 425.

    Death of the weaker of conjoined twins was inevitable at separation whereas the stronger was expected to survive. Without surgery, both were expected to die in infancy. Successful application, upheld on appeal, was made for a declaration that the operation might lawfully be carried out, notwithstanding parental opposition.

17. South Buckinghamshire NHS Trust v R (A Patient) [1996] 7 Med LR 401.

    23-year old existed in a 'low awareness state'. No obligation to treat if, in all the circumstances, life would be so afflicted as to be intolerable. See also (10) above where treatment withdrawal was justified on grounds of futility.

18. Wade DT, Johnston C. The permanent vegetative state. BMJ 1999 319:841.

    Review of clinical features plus practical guide on steps required to obtain court's approval to discontinue treatment.

19. Bliss MR. Brit Med J 2000 320:67.

    Critical analysis by a consultant geriatrician of the reprimand and suspension of a GP for ordering withdrawal of nutritional supplements from a demented elderly patient. Reported to police by nurses; police referred to GMC.

20. A National Health Service Trust v D and Ors [2000] Lloyd's Rep Med 411.

    Successful application by NHS Trust for a declaration that a 19-month old child with irreversible lung disease be treated in accordance with his best interests as judged by paediatrician responsible for his care, including non-resuscitation from cardiac or respiratory arrest. No infringement of right to life (European Convention on Human Rights, Article 2); right under Article 3 (no inhuman and degrading treatment) protected.

21. **NHS Trust A v Mrs M NHS Trust v Mrs H [2001] Lloyd's Med Law Rep 28.**

    Withdrawal of hydration and nutrition from patients in PVS was deemed by the President of the Family Division of the High Court not to contravene relevant Articles of the European Convention on Human Rights.

22. **Re J (A Minor) [1993] 4 Med LR 21.**

    Infant with profound neurological disability and frequent convulsions compromising respiration. Court of Appeal reversed a decision requiring that child be given life-prolonging treatment, including mechanical ventilation. There is no obligation to provide treatment which, in *bona fide* opinion of practitioner, is not in patient's best interests. 'Wholly inconsistent with the law' to order treatment contrary to doctor's clinical judgment.

23. **R v Portsmouth Hospital NHS Trust [1999] Lloyd's Rep Med 367.**

    Seriously disabled 12-year old given morphine against wishes of mother and a non-consensual DNR order was written. Violence followed between staff and family. Application for Judicial Review of the Trust's decision failed. Court of Appeal held it was inappropriate for court to declare what a hospital should or should not do as a matter of law. Individual cases of conflict should be resolved at the time by referral to Family Division of the High Court for declaration of child's best interests, or application under s8 Children's Act 1989, or make child a ward of court.

24. **Withholding and Withdrawing Life-prolonging Treatments: Good Practice in Decision-making. General Medical Council, August 2002.**

    Sets out guiding principles and describes their application in specific clinical circumstances.

25. **R v Bourne [1939] 1 KB 687.**

    Criminal prosecution for procuring a miscarriage. Not unlawful if done in good faith for sole purpose of preserving the life of the mother – interpreted to include adverse consequences to physical health short of death.

▶ Glossary of legal terms, phrases and abbreviations

Act of parliament:	completed parliamentary legislation
Actus reus:	factual element of a criminal offence
ADR:	Alternative Dispute Resolution – alternatives to litigation
Aggravated damages:	additional compensation for injurious personal conduct
Appellate Courts:	courts hearing appeals from decisions of a lower court or judicial officer
Assault:	threat causing apprehension of immediate physical contact
Battery:	non-consensual touching
Burden of proof:	party on whom onus lies to prove its case
CFA:	Conditional Fee Agreement
Civil law:	civil legal procedure derived from Roman law
CNST:	Clinical Negligence Scheme for Trusts
Common law:	body of decided English legal cases, ie 'caselaw'
Competence:	sufficiency of mental faculties to take legally valid decisions
Consideration:	the price of a contractual agreement
Contract:	a legally enforceable agreement
Damages:	financial compensation
ICAS:	Independent Complaints Advocacy Service
Inquest and inquisition:	proceedings and conclusion of coroner's court
Issue of proceedings:	first formal step in civil litigation
Judicial Review:	remedy for wrongful exercise of administrative power
Legal aid:	state funded financial assistance for legal proceedings
Limitation:	extinguishing of legal right of action by passage of time
Litigation Friend:	court-approved legal representative
LSC:	Legal Services Commission
MDOs:	Medical Defence Organisations

Mens rea:	a criminally culpable state of mind
Misadventure:	a sub-section of accident
Misfeasance:	wrong-doing
Multiplicand:	net annual value of an ongoing loss
Multiplier:	variable reflecting period of a loss, discounted for early receipt
NCAA:	National Clinical Assessment Authority
Neglect:	gross failure to provide basic necessities
Negligence:	culpable transgression of a duty
NHSLA:	National Health Service Litigation Authority
NPSA:	National Patient Safety Agency
PALS:	Patient Advocacy and Liaison Services
PCT:	Primary Care Trust
Parliamentary Bill:	a proposed item of parliamentary legislation
Particulars of Claim:	formal statement of claimant's case
Pleadings:	collection of formal documents encapsulating an action
	the term Statement of Case is now preferred
Precedent:	a binding judicial decision
Privy Council:	body of advisers to the Sovereign, appointed on the advice of Ministers
	Judicial Committee of Privy Council hears appeals, eg from professional disciplinary bodies
Proceedings:	formal legal action
Quantum:	the financial value of a claim for compensation
Res ipsa loquitur:	aphorism meaning 'the thing speaks for itself'
Service (of documents):	delivery by a legally accepted method
SHA:	Strategic Health Authority
Standard of proof:	degree of certainty to be achieved for an action to succeed
Statement of case:	term introduced by Civil Procedure Rules 1999 to replace Pleadings
Statute:	an Act of Parliament
Statutory Instrument:	subordinate (delegated) legislation permitted by a parent Act
Tort:	civil wrong-doing not including breach of contract
Vicarious liability:	liability for injury caused by another – eg an employee
VOICE:	National Commission for Patient and Public Involvement in Health

▶ Index